Hugh L. Dryden's Career in Aviation and Space

by
Michael H. Gorn

NASA History Office
Code ZH
NASA Headquarters
Washington, DC 20546

Monographs in
Aerospace History
Number 5
1996

Foreword

This account of the life of Dr. Hugh Latimer Dryden is especially appropriate now. The NASA Hugh L. Dryden Flight Research Center (DFRC) was named in his honor exactly 20 years ago. This year we also celebrate 50 years of flight research here. It is fitting that people associated with the Center, with NASA as a whole, and those outside of NASA who are interested in the history of aviation and space, be reminded of Hugh Dryden's enormous contributions.

Hugh Dryden was a research scientist of the highest order, an aeronautics pioneer, the Director of the National Advisory Committee for Aeronautics (NACA), and then the first NASA Deputy Administrator. Dr. Hugh Dryden's special relationship to the Dryden Flight Research Center goes far beyond its name. Among Hugh Dryden's first actions after becoming the NACA's Director of Research in September 1947, was to inform Walt Williams, the director of the flight research operation here in the desert, that the NACA Muroc organization, formed the previous year, would now become a permanent facility known as the NACA Muroc Flight Test Unit.

Hugh Dryden strongly supported the flight research conducted here with the early rocket-powered aircraft. He represented the NACA on the interagency Research Airplane Committee that supervised the beginnings of the critically important X-15 research at the High Speed Flight Station.

As Dr. Gorn recounts, Hugh Dryden had begun work in the transonic region very early in his career, and in fact it was he who coined the word "transonic," because no such word existed to describe speeds at or near that of sound in the early 1920s. Much of the research conducted here at the Center has concerned transonic flight, so that is another link between Dryden the man and Dryden the Center.

Dr. Gorn also describes Hugh Dryden's work with the "crucial transition from laminar to turbulent flow," another very important aspect of flight research here at DFRC over the five decades of its existence. This work continues today in the research being done on the F-16XL to examine Supersonic Laminar Flow Control—a project that would have been dear to the heart of Hugh Dryden.

Finally, Hugh Dryden wrote a description of flight research that has served ever since as the unofficial motto of the Center that bears his name and, in a very real sense, carries on his work. It separates, he stated, "the real from the imagined," and makes known the "overlooked and the unexpected." That brief line more effectively describes exactly what we do at the Dryden Flight Research Center than anything that has been written before or since.

For all of these reasons, I am very glad to have this story of the life of Hugh Dryden appear during the Dryden Flight Research Center's anniversary year. We at Dryden will look forward to the full length biography that Dr. Gorn is preparing to write as a follow-up to this shorter study. This account does a great service in bringing Hugh Dryden's accomplishments to light.

Kenneth J. Szalai
Director
Hugh L. Dryden Flight Research Center

Table of Contents

Introduction 1

Early Years 1

World War II 5

The NACA Years 7

The Transition from the NACA to NASA 11

Early NASA Years 13

Continued Service in NASA 15

Final Years 19

Notes 21

Key Documents 25

    1. The Nation's Manned Space Flights, 1 October 1965 26
    2. Joint US-USSR Talks on Cooperative Space Research Projects, Rome 1963. 45
    3. Hugh L. Dryden to Senator Robert S. Kerr, 22 June 1961. 66
    4. A National Space Program for the United States, Los Angeles, California, 26 April 1958. 68
    5. Scientists of Forty-Six Nations Study the Land, Sea, and Air Around Us, 16 April 1956. 83
    6. Trends in NACA Research and Development, Los Angeles, California, 5 October 1951. 91
    7. The Dawn of the Supersonic Age, Berkely 24 May 1948 and Los Angeles 25 May 1948. 106
    8. The Importance of Religion in American Life, 12 March 1950. 123

Index 131

Cover photo: NASA Photo EC96 43457-1, bust of Hugh Latimer Dryden unveiled at the ceremony on March 26, 1976, renaming the NASA Flight Research Center as the Hugh L. Dryden Flight Research Center. The bust is a cast of an original bronze by Una Hanbury, also dating from 1976. The copy now resides in building 4800 of the Dryden Flight Research Center. Photo by Dennis Taylor.

Design and layout: Steven Lighthill, Visual Information Specialist, Dryden Flight Research Center

Introduction

Hugh Latimer Dryden led a life rich in paradox. Born in obscurity, he attained international prominence. Indifferent to self-advancement, he nonetheless rose to the pinnacle of the aeronautics profession and subsequently assumed a pivotal role in the initial period of space exploration. Although a research scientist of the first order, he nurtured within himself a profoundly spiritual outlook.

Early Years

Hugh Dryden began his uncommon journey in remote and rural Worcester County, Maryland, at the southern tip of the state. His father, Samuel Isaac Dryden, renounced the farming tradition common to the Eastern Shore and taught school in Pocomoke City, one of the county's few population centers. Inhabited by only 1,000 people in the late 19th century, this working class town on the quiet Pocomoke River found itself isolated by crude roads and hard travel from the sophistication of Baltimore and Washington, D.C. Samuel Dryden married a local woman named Zenovia Hill Culver, and in an ambitious venture, turned from teaching to operating a general store at a country crossroads known as West Post Office. The young couple had three sons; the first was born on July 2, 1898, and named Hugh Latimer. Raymond followed soon after, and Leslie was born many years later.[1]

Like the rest of rural America at the turn of the century, the people of Worcester County lived in comparative isolation, but economic forces bound them to national and international financial events. Depressions often seized the country during the 19th century and another was suffered in 1901. Like earlier episodes, it spread extensive unrest and unemployment. In 1907, the nation experienced yet one more of these temblors when several of the large New York banks underwent runs on their assets because of their speculative excesses. To repay depositors, loans were called in throughout the country, credit contracted everywhere, and many businesses failed.

Samuel Dryden suffered a hard fate in the Panic of 1907, one that transformed his family's fortunes. The elder Dryden had to abandon his general store and decided to start afresh with his wife and sons in Baltimore. For him, this move symbolized the end of ambition; he found work as a streetcar conductor and remained one the rest of his life.

For young Hugh Dryden, Baltimore opened opportunities that were unthinkable in Southern Maryland. Indeed, in the big city he showed extraordinary promise. He entered Baltimore City College (a high school, despite its name) and received his diploma at age 14, the youngest ever to graduate. Not merely the youngest, he ranked first in a class of 172 and won the Peabody Prize for excellence in mathematics.

If not a prodigy, then certainly highly precocious, the quiet and diligent student continued to blossom. Despite slender family resources, he received admission (on scholarship) to Johns Hopkins, the university founded by Baltimore's famous Quaker merchant. Dryden proved himself especially gifted in physics and mathematics and began advanced study with Professor Joseph Ames, an important figure on campus. Ames not only headed the Physics Department but also eventually became President of Johns Hopkins. More important to Dryden's development, his professor would one day chair the National Advisory Committee for Aeronautics (NACA), an institution at the vanguard of aircraft research. In Dryden, Ames had discovered a star pupil, whom he called, "the brightest young man [I] ever had, without exception." He took his Bachelor's degree with honors in three years and in 1918 completed a Masters thesis etitled "Airplanes: An Introduction to the Physical Principles Embodied in their Use." Ames had introduced Dryden to a subject that would occupy the rest of his life.[2]

Hugh Dryden at age 17 as he appeared in the Johns Hopkins yearbook ca. 1917. (NASA photo 76-H-545 from a Johns Hopkins University original)

Certain of Ames' encouragement and assistance, Dryden decided to work toward his doctorate. Two obstacles blocked the way: lack of money and the military draft. The United States entered World War I in April 1917, but only in the desperate Battle of the Marne the following year did American forces suffer heavy losses. Ultimately, about 50,000 U.S. soldiers died on or over the fields of France. Dryden faced conscription but was spared the dangers and disruptions because of age; the Selective Service Act of 1917 exempted young men until their twenty-first birthday. He would be safe until July 1919.

Ames found a means by which Dryden could satisfy both his patriotic instincts and his need for cash. The professor had placed several of his students at the National Bureau of Standards (NBS) in suburban Maryland and in June 1918 found a summer job for Hugh as an inspector of munitions gauges. Dryden accepted gratefully, expecting to return to school in the fall. While the position entailed a long train ride each day and a streetcar connection enroute from Baltimore to the Bureau, it also opened some fine opportunities. Within weeks, Ames persuaded Dryden to transfer to the Bureau's new Aerodynamics Section, at the heart of which stood one of the nation's first wind tunnels. More important, the Johns Hopkins professor now appeared regularly in Washington on NACA business and took the occasion to offer courses to his NBS students. Dryden could thus work a full schedule at NBS (for the salary of $100 a month) and use the wind tunnel for after hours doctoral research under Ames' watchful eye.

Dryden wasted no time. In spring 1919, he received the Ph.D. degree in applied physics, at 20 the youngest person ever to earn a Johns Hopkins University doctorate. His dissertation, titled "Air Forces on Circular Cylinders" described the scale effects of air flowing around columns perpendicular to the wind and launched him in the rising field of aerodynamics.[3]

Not content merely to receive his doctorate and obtain his first professional position before he could vote, Dryden experienced equally noteworthy events in 1920. In January of that year, he married Mary Libbie Travers, a young woman he had met some years before at Sunday School in the Appold Methodist Church, Baltimore. Outgoing and fun-loving, she provided counterpoint to her young husband's reserved and laconic manner, perhaps somewhat mitigating his ways over the years. At first, they lived in Baltimore, but when he awoke one evening in New Jersey after falling asleep on the homeward bound train, they decided to relocate their household to Washington, D.C. Finally, during the same year, he won promotion to Chief of the Aerodynamics Section and henceforth directed the Bureau's wind-tunnel research and operations.[4]

Dryden's scientific standing rested largely on the theoretical insights, the experiments, and the publications dating from his first six years in this position. Very early in his tenure, he selected the field of high-speed aerodynamics, concentrating on problems associated with flight at or near the speed of sound. Because almost no one had yet studied velocities in this range, the choice suggests the audacity of youth. Indeed, when he began his inquiries in 1920, the winner of the Schneider Cup Race—a competition among the fastest aircraft in the world, pressed to their limits—flew at a mere 107 miles per hour.

Nonetheless, working with his friend, mentor, and the future director of NBS Dr. Lyman Briggs, Dryden sought to unravel the strange phenomenon known as compressibility. At the time, it denoted unexplained boundary-layer separation and buffet encountered by propeller tips rotating at very high speeds. The problem arose as engines of increasing power drove the blades faster and faster. The Dryden-Briggs research was conducted at large compressor plants during the mid-1920s because wind tunnels could not yet supply the needed velocity. This research resulted in some of the first experimental observations of aerodynamic drag approaching the speed of sound, in very early insights regarding the effects of compressibility on lift and drag, and in invaluable data for propeller manufacturers designing high velocity airfoils. Dryden and Briggs' findings also stimulated additional transonic research and ultimately prompted the construction of supersonic wind tunnels capable of testing theoretical design concepts applicable not only to aircraft but later to rockets and missiles. He and Briggs obtained the first U.S. wind-tunnel data showing lift and drag for airfoils above the speed of sound. Thus, the young physicist quickly established his reputation.

Dryden attracted yet more notice with his breakthroughs in wind-tunnel design. In the late 1920s, he and A.M. Kuethe, a Bureau colleague, discovered a dilemma: an airship model had been

Dryden at 30 ca. 1928. (NASA photo 76-H-546 from a Johns Hopkins University original)

tested at both the NBS wind tunnel and the one at the Navy Yard in Washington, D.C. The drag data results were 100 percent at odds with each other.

To quantify accuracy, Dryden and his associate employed a hot wire anemometer, rigged ingeniously to measure rapid air fluctuations. They discovered that even slight variations in turbulence inside wind tunnels could cause large experimental discrepancies. Using the special anemometer, Dryden redesigned existing facilities to help compensate for such differences and also suggested new methods of wind tunnel construction that would greatly reduce incidental turbulence.

His research benefitted from these more nearly accurate and consistent instruments. These instruments allowed him to observe with great precision the crucial transition from laminar to turbulent flow within the boundary layer. The application of more exacting measurements, in turn, opened the way for wing and propeller designs that maximized laminar flow, thus reducing drag.[5] More importantly, his findings verified experimentally the pivotal laminar flow concepts theorized in 1907 by the German Ludwig Prandtl, thus winning for Dryden wide acclaim among the world's aerodynamics practitioners.

Yet paradoxically, his daily routine at the NBS increasingly involved not only basic research but also a wide variety of engineering projects. During the late 1920s, he investigated the effects of wind pressures on skyscrapers and chimneys. During the early 1930s he found himself leading a classic Depression-era inquiry on new materials and techniques for low-cost housing. The young physicist also became active in automotive streamlining and even researched water circulation in the plumbing of the Empire State Building.

Despite the heavy load of solutions-oriented research, which diverted him from (but did not prevent) the pursuit of fundamental studies in his chosen field, Dryden remained at NBS. In fact, he undertook these new assignments with the same firm purpose as ever. Perhaps the needs of a growing family suppressed any secret desires for more basic research. Hugh, Jr., was born in 1923 and Mary Ruth arrived two years later. The economic hardships of the time may also have bred a degree of caution. More likely, though, Hugh Dryden's personality and religious frame of reference anchored him to NBS. Genuinely self-effacing, his instincts revolted against careerism and self-promotion. Just as compelling, his private yet intense spirituality—he had been a lay Methodist minister since his teens—rendered him all but deaf to the call of ambition. In any event, he worked steadily and diligently at the Bureau, impressing his colleagues as much with his modesty as his intellect.

Dryden rose in rank almost in spite of himself. In 1934, he became Chief of the Mechanics and Sound Division, which included his own Aerodynamics Section.[6] This promotion seemed to inaugurate a cascade of recognition, both in America and abroad. First, he was elected to the Philosophical Society of Washington and became a Fellow of the American Association for the Advancement of Science. Then in 1934, he travelled to Europe to present a paper at the Fourth International Congress of Applied Mechanics. Entitled

"Boundary Layer Flow Near Flat Plates," it further enhanced Dryden's standing because of its significant contribution to describing the mechanics of laminar flow. Two years later *Aerodynamic Theory*, a book of essays by the most eminent international authorities, rolled off the presses in Berlin and included a section by Dryden on aerodynamic cooling. Finally, to crown these remarkable years, in 1938 he was invited to deliver the Wilbur Wright Lecture sponsored by the Institute of the Aeronautical Sciences, the first American so honored. He presented a magisterial survey of the existing state of research in a lecture called "Turbulence and the Boundary Layer." The Bureau responded to this extraordinary chain of professional successes by naming Dryden its Chief Physicist.[7]

World War II

When Dryden celebrated his 40th birthday in July 1938, he unknowingly neared another milestone. Like millions of others, his path would be refracted by war. Events in Europe and Asia portended another worldwide conflict and a sharp rise in military projects at the Bureau confirmed it. Until now, his career entailed the management of small numbers of technical people who used relatively simple equipment to arrive at narrowly defined objectives. He knew every member of his staff, their work, and their capacities. Shortly, he found himself directing large numbers of people from a variety of institutions, commanding an impressive array of resources, and assuming responsibility for undertakings of the highest national importance.[8]

The venerable NACA opened these opportunities for Dryden and many others. In 1940 its new chairman, Dr. Vannevar Bush, directed NACA's Executive Secretary John F. Victory to draft congressional legislation for a National Defense Research Committee. The proposal would systematically enlist and employ civilian scientists in the war effort. When the idea bore fruit in the creation of the Office of Scientific Research and Development (OSRD), Bush left the NACA to head OSRD. Shortly after his arrival, a call was issued for scientists to discuss the feasibility of guided missiles. Because of his fame in aerodynamics, Dryden assumed a leading role. Meantime, the U.S. Navy's Bureau of Ordnance reckoned the potential military value of such weapons and assembled a group of its own employees, as well as a cadre of professors from the Massachusetts Institute of Technology. The OSRD leaders asked Dryden to take charge of this group, known as the Bureau of Ordnance Experimental Unit. Headquartered at the NBS, the project also incorporated Dryden's own staff.

For much of World War II, Dryden immersed himself in the immense task of conceiving, designing, testing, and finally procuring operational units for the Navy. The sense of wartime emergency added to the pressure. Dryden found relief from these demands—as well as delight—in the birth of his third child, Nancy, who arrived in 1940.

The missile, called the Bat, consisted of an aircraft-launched gravity bomb capable of self-correction in flight. As transmitters in its front end beamed radar waves to enemy vessels, a receiver (also embedded in the Bat) picked up the reflected pulses and sent appropriate signals to the missile's control surfaces, steering it toward the target. Bomber crews could thus release the weapon from a considerable distance and fly away with the confidence that the weapon would reach the target on its own. To realize this great advance in naval warfare, Dryden divided his researchers in three categories: Navy personnel for munitions development and testing (on barges in Chesapeake Bay and on Liberty Ships in the Atlantic), the M.I.T. contingent for homing system experiments, and the NBS team for aerodynamics work. Despite formidable technical and administrative obstacles, Dryden and the Bat enjoyed a significant success. Indeed, although several automatic guided missiles were developed by the U.S. during the war, only the Bat proved effective under fire. It appeared first in the Pacific in April 1945 at the Battle of Okinawa. Aircraft of Fleet Wing One not only sank several Japanese ships with the new weapon but also employed it successfully against land targets.[9]

Fresh from the experience of guided missile development, Dryden undertook a second wartime assignment. In the fall of 1944 he received a call for assistance from long-time friend and colleague, Dr. Theodore von Kármán, a man known as much for wit and charm as for brilliance. The world-renowned Hungarian physicist had been persuaded by Commanding General of the Army Air Forces Henry H. Arnold to lead a group of scientists to Europe to assess war-related breakthroughs in flight. Dr. von Kármán reluctantly agreed and turned to his trusted confidant Hugh Dryden to be his partner. They faced great challenges. General Arnold ascribed the highest national importance to their mission, demanding not just a report on the *existing* state of aeronautical knowledge with Pearl Harbor in mind, he also wanted a *forecast of long-range developments* necessary to prevent (or deter) future devastating air attacks on American cities. Beginning in December 1944, Dryden would devote the better part of a year assisting von Kármán in this endeavor.

During several months of preparation in the Pentagon Dryden and von Kármán assembled some of the nation's most able figures in the various flight sciences. The team, known collectively as the Army Air Forces Scientific Group, departed in April 1945 to Europe, with hopes of visiting the U.S.S.R. as well. In London, Dryden and von Kármán donned uniforms bearing the simulated ranks of colonel and major general, respectively, and moved forward to Paris. They advanced to the German border and crossed it on learning of a highly secret aeronautics laboratory just unearthed at Braunschweig. This complex, brilliantly concealed in a setting of woods and farms, had been reduced to ruins by the invading U.S. troops. Dryden interviewed many of the remaining scientists about their projects and pored over technical data relating to swept-wing aerodynamics, high-speed human physiology, and other surprising research. He then parted from von Kármán and traveled to Munich, where Dr. Wernher von Braun, General Walter

Dryden, Dr. Ben Lockspeiser (Great Britain), Theodore von Kármán, and Dr. A.P. Rowe (Great Britain) in occupied Germany, 9 May, 1945. (NASA photo 76-H-547 from a Johns Hopkins University original)

Dornberger, and some 400 scientists of the Peenemünde rocket facility had been relocated. There Dryden conducted intense interrogations about the V-1 cruise missile and the V-2 ballistic missile. Meanwhile, von Kármán flew to Moscow, and Dryden returned to Germany to finish the job. At one point, his quiet but determined style was put to the test. When he discovered an uncrated Swiss wind tunnel, he pressed to have it shipped immediately to Wright Field for investigation. Despite the crush of transatlantic air freight, he proved persuasive; precious space was found on a B-17 bomber. After further exploratory trips to the United Kingdom (U.K.), Switzerland, and France, Dryden returned home.

The whole Scientific Advisory Group reunited in Washington, D.C., that summer to draft *Where We Stand*, which recounted the existing state of air power technology. A second foreign tour then got underway, to Europe again and to Asia. Once it was completed, General Arnold would receive his much anticipated long-range forecast. Rather than travel with the others, Hugh Dryden remained in Washington to act as general editor of the ensuing report, which was due to the general on December 15, 1945. During November and early December the task all but inundated him. In just a few weeks the 25 contributors produced 33 essays, all requiring Dryden's close scrutiny for unifying conceptual themes, technical accuracy, and substantive editing. As he finished, he cabled each article to von Kármán, who had remained in Paris to write a long introductory essay titled "Science, the Key to Air Supremacy." Along with the rest, Dryden also reviewed the text of his great friend and managed to write two sections himself on guided missiles. The resulting thirteen volumes—known together as *Toward New Horizons*—touched on every aspect of air power research, from aerodynamics to propulsion, from fuels to radar. It made a lasting impression on General Arnold and the U.S. Army Air Forces. Thanks in large part to Dryden's exacting standards of scientific rigor, logical consistency, and written clarity, the conclusions imparted one clear and lasting thought to the Army Air Forces (and later to the U.S. Air Force): To deter attack, modern air power required the constant application of the latest and best scientific thinking. For his labors he received the National Medal of Freedom from President Truman.[10]

The NACA Years

Dryden returned to the NBS upon completion of *Toward New*

Horizons, but like so many scientists who engaged in war-related research and administration, he had substantially outgrown his old responsibilities. Whether he sought it or not, the war had earned him a stature of consequence in aeronautics, and this new standing received almost immediate recognition. In January 1946, he became the Bureau's Assistant Director and six months later, its Associate Director. Yet soon and suddenly, Dryden's career attained full flower. Since 1919, the formidable engineer George W. Lewis had been the NACA's Director of Aeronautical Research, its chief of day-to-day operations. The organization multiplied during World War II: from 500 employees in 1939 to 6,000 in 1945 and from one laboratory when he began to five research facilities shortly after the war. Lewis' health collapsed under the exertions associated with the NACA's wartime responsibilities, and in 1947 his resignation became imminent. When the NACA Main Committee (its governing board) met in Washington, D.C., to consider successors, they found a leading candidate close at hand. Few could match Dryden's record of sparkling scientific achievement and wide administrative experience. Hugh Dryden assumed the position in September, becoming perhaps the most influential civilian figure in American flight research.[11]

High-speed wind tunnel at Langley Memorial Aeronautical Laboratory, Langley Field, VA. (NASA photo LMAL 28410)

Dryden's new importance rested in part on the very size and superiority of the NACA's physical plant, which constituted a sort of legacy from Lewis to Dryden. The first field location had arisen on remote marsh land in Hampton, Virginia, and opened in 1920. By the 1930s, the Langley Memorial Aeronautical Laboratory housed a full-scale wind tunnel and many other unique pieces of research equipment. Nonetheless, striking European aeronautical advances before World War II prompted Congress to allocate funds for the NACA's expansion. Gradually, Langley doubled its capacity to undertake new projects. In the meantime, an immense laboratory was planned for Moffett Field near San Francisco, California. Designed to augment the aeronautical research of West Coast aircraft manufacturers, the facilities built in 1939 and 1940, became known as the Ames Aeronautical Laboratory (for Dryden's mentor Joseph Ames). Its 12

NACA 16-foot wind tunnel at Ames Aeronautical Laboratory, Moffett Field, CA. (NASA photo)

by 24 meter wind tunnel dwarfed the former world's champion at Langley. In 1940, yet another impressive center, this one devoted to propulsion, received congressional approval. Upon the death of George Lewis in 1948, this facility erected in Cleveland, Ohio, assumed the name of the Lewis Flight Propulsion Laboratory. Finally, two test operations came into being. To explore flight characteristics in the transonic range, a former naval station overlooking Chesapeake Bay was pressed into service as the Pilotless Aircraft Research Station at Wallops Island, Virginia in 1945. To gather flight data on transonic and high-velocity experimental aircraft, the NACA opened the Muroc Flight Test Unit in 1946 on the dry lakebed near the desert outpost of Mojave, California. After 1954, this unit was renamed the NACA High Speed Flight Station.

Yet the wind tunnels, runways, test stands, hangars, and fabrication shops that comprised the NACA in 1947 accounted for only a part of Lewis' legacy to Dryden. Perhaps to a greater degree, the NACA's strength lay in its unusual staff. In the face of the Great Depression, many of the nation's best young aeronautical engineering minds turned to the NACA for relatively secure employment. The work was not just steady, but interesting. Before World War II, the NACA concentrated on theoretical studies and basic aerodynamic research. Once the United States joined the conflict, it concentrated on drag "cleanup" for American aircraft. The contributions before and during the war were immense. A family of pioneering airfoil shapes, cowlings for radial engines, and imaginative wind-tunnel types and designs only begin to express the achievements. Even more than these advances, the body of knowledge contained in the NACA technical publications had become an international standard for aeronautics research. It also employed such genuine luminaries in the aerodynamics profession as Max Munk, Fred Weick, Eastman Jacobs, Richard Whitcomb, Robert T. Jones, and John Stack.[12]

Hugh Dryden, Director of NACA preparing to board a Lockheed Constellation enroute to give the 37th Wilbur Wright Lecture before the Royal Aeronautical Society, Egland, in April 1949. (NASA photo 76-H-549 from a Johns Hopkins University original)

Yet, the NACA directed by Hugh Dryden (after 1949 as Director rather than simply Director of Research) would differ from that of his predecessor. The new research director did have extensive administrative experience but regarded himself principally as a scientist among scientists, one who pointed his staff and his agency toward new discoveries. Indeed, at the time of assuming his duties, he had already been editor of *The Journal of the Institute of the Aeronautical Sciences* for six years (a post he continued to fill until 1956). In addition Dryden helped found and sat on the board of editors of *The Quarterly of Applied Mechanics*. As readers of these publications knew, Dryden had devoted his entire research career to high-speed flight. Now, he would lead the NACA in this direction. He took courage in this objective in October 1947 when he learned, just after arriving at the NACA, that Captain Charles E.

Yeager had flown a rocket-powered aircraft past the speed of sound. The event gave Dryden occasion to state clearly the NACA's future course:

> During the first 25 years—until World War II—most of the NACA's research was concentrated on aerodynamic problems... [and] the NACA produced a wealth of information that was used to good advantage by America's aircraft industry. This was a course of action that paid handsome dividends, in directly useful information, on the taxpayers' investment. The NACA's effort in World War II was devoted largely to applied research, the business of finding 'quick fixes' to improve the performance of existing airplanes and to make production engines more powerful. By the close of World War II, the end had come for development of the airplane as conceived by the Wright Brothers. Now, it was possible to build useful rocket engines, and with this development came the possibility of flight at velocities exceeding the speed of sound and to altitudes higher than the earth's atmosphere.[13]

Dryden turned immediately to constructing the necessary infrastructure to achieve his goal. Wind tunnels capable of simulating velocities up to ten times Mach 1 now became imperative and national figures, such as Air Force Secretary W. Stuart Symington, supported the idea (although more for reasons of Cold War superiority than scientific inquiry). Nonetheless, Congress voted for a National Unitary Wind Tunnel Plan shaped by Dryden's vision of aeronautical research, which allocated these immense and costly resources on a systematic basis and distributed them equitably among the NACA and the U.S. Air Force for supersonic and hypersonic testing. This task completed, Dryden and his laboratories concerned themselves with flight vehicles. Before and during the 1950s, the NACA made invaluable aerodynamics contributions to the USAF high-velocity Century Series fighter aircraft. In 1954, he assumed the chairmanship of the new Air Force-Navy-NACA Research Airplane Committee. This group surveyed the data from such experimental programs as the X-1, X-2, X-3, X-4, X-5, YF-92A, D-558-1 and -2 and conceived of the hypersonic X-15 rocket plane. Dryden provided more than a guiding hand in the deliberations. Year after year, in a time of

NACA Executive Committee meeting at Langley Research Center June 2, 1950. (NASA photo)

NACA meeting at Lewis Laboratory, October 1957. (NASA photo)

pinched budgets, he achieved consistent congressional support for the X-15 during the early National Aeronautics and Space Administration (NASA) period (see below). Eventually flying as fast as 4,520 miles per hour and as high as 67 miles above the planet, the X-15 program lent a solid technical basis to the early U.S. human space program, embodied in Project Mercury. (See below for a discussion of the more purely aeronautical results of the X-15 flight research.) Finally, the NACA Director pressed for solutions to the problem of re-entry heating encountered by vehicles such as missiles, aircraft, and capsules, penetrating the atmosphere from high altitudes. The NACA scientists found answers in the blunt body shape discovered by H. Julian Allen of the Ames Laboratory and in the principle of ablation resulting from the materials research of Robert Gilruth at Langley.

Dryden's earliest and clearest position on fully realized space flight occurred in 1955 after his election as Home Secretary of the National Academy of Sciences. In this capacity, he was asked to review satellite programs proposed for the International Geophysical Year (IGY). Skeptical of expensive and unproven ventures, the NACA Director at first balked at the requested $100 million annual appropriation (which, after all, rivalled the entire yearly budget of the NACA). He relented once a set of clear scientific objectives had been formulated. Under his direction, the NACA assisted the IGY projects significantly. The Langley Laboratory formed a Satellite Vehicle Group to explore spacecraft structures, trajectories, and guidance; its Pilotless Aircraft Research Division initiated rocket studies.

Thus, by the mid-1950s Dryden had accustomed the NACA to the idea that high-speed research and, ultimately, space endeavors loomed large and would assume even greater importance in time. Of course, in 1957 Dryden still focused his organization's 8,000 employees mainly on atmospheric flight. Although he had shifted an increasing part of his staff and resources to space-related projects, until a firm national commitment to space exploration emerged, Dryden and the NACA—whose final A, after all, stood for *aeronautics*—could only accomplish limited objectives in research and flight outside the atmosphere. Once the President and Congress gave their assent, however, Hugh Dryden could summon within his organization a cadre of experienced scientists and engineers able to assume pivotal roles in the new endeavor.[14]

The Transition from the NACA to NASA

Of course, the spur to space came not from within the U.S. but from outside it. The launch of the Soviet Sputnik I satellite on October 4, 1957, released almost palpable shock waves across the country. At once, Sputnik represented not only the capacity of a hostile power to fly without challenge over American territory; it also destroyed the complacent belief that U.S. technology surpassed all others. Amplified by sensational reports in the press, the distant signals from the little sphere in orbit rang like trumpets in the ears of the President, members of Congress, and military leaders.

Dryden, his headquarters staff, and the NACA laboratories did not share the nation's panic. They knew the Soviets had the capacity to launch a satellite, an objective declared publicly by the Russians earlier in 1957. This flight would be their contribution to IGY; the U.S. promised a similar feat with Project Vanguard. Dryden also realized the NACA's ten years of achievement in high-speed flight left the institution better prepared than any other to participate in whatever space policy might emerge after Sputnik.

Yet, in a case of high irony, despite his long and vigorous pursuit of preliminary space research, Dryden himself fell victim to the Sputnik hysteria. He became identified in the newspapers and in Congress with the scientific establishment, which somehow had allowed Sputnik to happen. Dryden, however, did little to cast off the false characterization. His plain, unassuming style and disdain for self-commendation attracted few allies in a time of loud accusations and expansive promises. Indeed, the political climate suggested a new set of personalities, unattached to the perceived shortcomings of past years, for leadership in space. Thus, during the 12 months of deliberations about an institutional response to Sputnik, Hugh Dryden was consulted and considered for a role of leadership; was not only heard, but heeded. Yet, his ultimate role turned out to be smaller than expected.[15]

Dryden (seated, second from left) with the House Select Committee on Astronautics and Space Exploration in April 1958, at hearings concerning the creation of NASA. (NASA photo 76-H-550 from a Johns Hopkins University original)

The National Aeronautics and Space Act (which became law in July 1958) and its offspring—the National Aeronautics and Space Administration—owed much to Dryden's efforts. Many government entities vied for control of the space mission: the Air Force, the Army, the Department of Defense's Advanced Research Projects Agency (ARPA), the Atomic Energy Commission, and the NACA itself. To choose among the candidates, President Eisenhower directed his Science Advisory Committee to review the various administrative options and make recommendations. On it sat two NACA figures of recognized competence and reputation: Hugh Dryden and the new chairman of the Main Committee, General Jimmy Doolittle. Together, they successfully lobbied the President's science advisors for a civilian space agency based on the NACA as its organizational core. They also testified before Congress, outlining the new agency's budget and span of operations, then stamping both with the NACA imprimatur.

As these consultations proceeded, Dryden prepared his staff and laboratories for their vastly expanded field of action, which they had already begun to explore. He formed a Special Committee on Space Technology chaired by an associate from *Toward New Horizons* days, Professor H. Guyford Stever of M.I.T. Members included such notables as James A. Van Allen, Wernher von Braun, H. Julian Allen, and William Pickering. Dryden also took administrative steps in anticipation of passage of the July law. Guessing what lay ahead, he asked Robert Gilruth and a Langley team to plan for human spaceflight. He also persuaded Abe Silverstein, the Assistant Director of the Lewis Laboratory, to transfer to Washington and assume the task of structurally transforming the NACA into NASA.

In the end, Dryden would oversee neither Gilruth's nor Silverstein's labors. This job would be assumed by T. Keith Glennan, President of the Case Institute of Technology and President Eisenhower's nominee to be NASA's first Administrator. Glennan agreed to come to Washington only on the condition that Hugh Dryden serve as his deputy. After 40 full years of government service, Dryden concealed his disappointment and continued to serve the public.[16]

Early NASA Years

Now 60 years of age, Dryden still had much to offer, and Glennan sorely needed his help. More than anyone, Dryden knew every corner of the former NACA, from its personalities to its technical capacity, from its budgetary practices to its institutional peculiarities. More vital still, he possessed as complete a knowledge of early space endeavors as anyone in America. Indeed, he had been responsible for or associated with almost all such efforts. Dryden had also developed through the years a finely tuned instinct for wise bureaucratic choices, honed in hours before congressional committees and sharpened in countless White House meetings. Finally, and perhaps most important of all, Hugh Dryden was known universally. Because of his prominence in such societies as the International Union of Theoretical and Applied Mechanics, of which he had been both president and vice-president, and his distinguished scientific research, he had perhaps as many contacts overseas as at home. In the United States, he knew just about every major, and many minor, figures in the field, including aircraft manufacturers, airline executives, airframe designers, test pilots, university scientists, and military officers.[17] So Keith Glennan, a distinguished highly capable engineer and administrator in his own right, began his tenure at NASA with perhaps his best decision: his choice of deputy.

The titular transformation of the NACA to NASA occurred on October 1, 1958. The actual realignments stretched on for two years and fell mostly to Dryden. Forming a single, cohesive entity from many constituent parts called forth some of the deputy administrator's best qualities: calmness under pressure, intensity in powers of analysis, and clarity of mind that remained fixed on the critical objectives despite any distractions of the moment. The Army held two of the most important pieces of the emerging mosaic. Together, these facilities had answered Sputnik 1 in January 1958 with America's first Earth satellite, Explorer 1. Despite Army objections, the Jet Propulsion Laboratory (JPL) left military cognizance on the last day of 1958. At the same time, an Executive Order assigned to NASA the Army contract with the California Institute of Technology, which provided for JPL staffing and operations. Army brass resisted more strenuously the loss of a part of its Ballistic Missile Agency in Huntsville, Alabama—the Development Operations Division, under the direction of Wernher von Braun, employing some 4,000 scientists and engineers. Nonetheless, after much bureaucratic scuffling, in March 1960 it too was transferred to NASA. With it came the prize of prizes: the gigantic Saturn booster project. Dryden also negotiated with the Defense Department a series of understandings on launch support and astronaut training. In addition he arranged for the gradual assumption by NASA of such crucial programs as the Air Force's F-1 rocket engine. The Navy's Project Vanguard and ARPA's space science projects also found homes at NASA. Finally, Dryden exercised a nurturing hand in establishing at Greenbelt, Maryland, the Robert H. Goddard Space Flight Center to launch and track unpiloted space vehicles and to develop space science experiments.[18]

Having locked NASA's structural components in place, Dryden spent the next years in somewhat contradictory pursuits: on the one hand advising and guiding those who planned the human missions that ultimately overtook the Soviet lead in space and, on the other, negotiating patiently and effectively with Soviet representatives for cooperation in space. His extensive international experience with professional societies prepared him well for diplomatic service. He first acted as Alternate Representative for Ambassador Henry Cabot Lodge to the United Nations Ad Hoc Committee on the Peaceful Uses of Outer Space. "I served," he later recalled, "on the technical subcommittee, and had the opportunity to prepare with some of my colleagues a report on the technical aspects of space technology." In fact, his activities resulted in a NASA invitation to other countries to undertake joint space research projects of mutual interest. Dryden then became chief negotiator during direct talks with the U.S.S.R. With his counterpart, Academician Anatoly A. Blagonravov, he signed limited, but nevertheless unprecedented, agreements on meteorology, communications, and magnetic field data. Dryden insisted on, and achieved, exchanges which provided clear mutual benefits. He likewise pressed for understandings with the U.K., Canada, Italy, and other nations to share information derived from space. "I am persuaded," he said, "that there are very great values to the United States in this cooperation."[19]

At the same time, Dryden laid the foundation for American leadership in space. All through the early months of Glennan's term, the headquarters staff undertook the burdensome task of long-range planning. The resulting Ten Year Plan—in which Dryden played an indispensable part—proposed expenditures of one to two billion annually and an average of two launches per month. Luckily, a reversal of fortune occurred in the sky, lending credence to the expansive projections. During 1959, seven of seventeen U.S. launches failed, but then, the program righted itself. Explorer 6 went into orbit and functioned perfectly. Pioneer 5 embarked toward Venus and ultimately relayed planetary data from as far as 22 million miles away. Tiros 1 captured thousands of photographs of the Earth's weather. In addition, in August 1960, Echo 1 unfolded in orbit to become the world's first passive communications satellite. The greatest challenge still awaited: To launch humans, not just machines, into space. Dryden followed the unveiling of the Ten Year Plan with an announcement to the NASA Industry Plans Conference that Project Mercury, the first U.S. program for launching humans into space, would be followed by a more ambitious one named Project Apollo.

Continued Service in NASA

But would Hugh Dryden participate in these activities, or retire at last? Toward the end of 1960, his period of office-holding appeared to be drawing to a close. John F. Kennedy narrowly defeated Richard M. Nixon for the presidency in November and all the executive appointees, including Keith Glennan, submitted their resignations. The deputy administrator also handed in his letter, but since the Kennedy transition office never acknowledged it, he stayed on in a caretaker capacity until the new administration selected its nominee.[20] Unfortunately, during the period of transition NASA came under sudden attack. The President-elect's Ad Hoc Space Panel, led by Dr. Jerome Wiesner, the White House Science Advisor-designate, issued a report sharply critical of the U.S. aeronautics, space, and missile programs. Naturally, the committee's recommendations were not free of political coloration; while he headed the Ad Hoc Panel, Wiesner also chaired the Democratic Party's Science Committee. Moreover during the year before the election, the Democratic candidate warned repeatedly of unfavorable space and missile "gaps" between American and Russian capabilities. Once elected, the winning party felt obliged to pinpoint the causes of the alleged inadequacies. These charges were published in the pages of the *New York Times*, which reprinted the Wiesner Report. It cited:

> 1. "A number of organizational and management deficiencies as well as problems of staffing and direction."
>
> 2. Duplication between NASA and the military space programs arising especially from rocket and ballistic missile research.
>
> 3. Flaws in the technical aspects of Project Mercury.
>
> 4. Neglect of aerodynamics research.
>
> 5. The exclusion of university and industrial scien-

tists from NASA activities.

6. A preoccupation with in-house research at the expense of private sector cooperation.

7. Lack of vision in the selection of science missions and errors in the selection of scientists to achieve them.

Undoubtedly, these accusations stung Dryden. As NACA Director and NASA Deputy Administrator over the past thirteen years, he had been perhaps more responsible than anyone for the policies criticized by Wiesner. He had worked tirelessly, often brilliantly—and always unobtrusively—to move aeronautics toward the margins of space. Although politics may have motivated some of the complaints, most of them accurately reflected an institution in the process of metamorphosis, from a laboratory operation to one based on contracts administration. On the other hand, some of the report's charges, especially those relating to civilian versus military roles and the long-term objectives in space, required decisions at the highest levels of government. Indeed, they awaited action by President Kennedy himself.

Be this as it may, in one area—Dryden's own specialty, aeronautics—the criticism in the Wiesner report was clearly inaccurate. Although in the wake of Sputnik the former aeronautical laboratories and facilities of the NACA had shifted much of their emphasis from pure aeronautics to the problems of space travel, they had by no means neglected aerodynamics research.

At Langley, for example, in the early 1950s, aerodynamicists had studied the variable-sweep wing as a way to improve the operating efficiency of a military aircraft. The NACA High Speed Flight Station had flight tested the concept on the X-5 from 1952 to 1955. The NACA researchers had subsequently identified a solution to changes in stability as the wings rotated through various angles of sweep. Wind-tunnel tests at Langley led the Department of Defense in 1961 to approve production of the first U.S. variable-sweep fighter, the F-111. Many subsequent military aircraft incorporated the concept.[21] This important aerodynamic discovery was continuing during the very years of transition from the NACA to NASA that the Wiesner Report purported to examine.

To give but one of many other examples of continued pathbreaking research in aerodynamics, as already noted the X-15 flight research was also beginning during Glennan's administration of NASA. The implications of that program for space were highly

James E. Webb, NASA Administrator, and Hugh L. Dryden, Deputy Administrator, appear before the Honorable Overton Brooks, Chairman of the House Committee on Science and Astronautics on March 13, 1961. (NASA photo 61-Admin.-9)

significant, but flight research had only begun in 1959. Thus its significance for both aeronautics and space could not be fully appreciated in early 1961 when the Wiesner Report appeared. Nevertheless, the X-15 airplane had been on the drawing board since 1954. By the end of 1960, the aircraft had already completed 31 flights at the NASA Flight Research Center in the Mojave Desert. Those knowledgeable about the program could already anticipate the enormous fund of data the aircraft would provide in such areas as hypersonic air flow, aerodynamic heating, control and stability of flight at hypersonic speeds (above Mach 5), reaction controls for flight above the atmosphere, transition from aerodynamic to reaction controls, piloting techniques for reentry, human factors, and flight instrumentation. These data significantly modified existing aerodynamic theory, especially in the areas of heat flow and wind-tunnel testing, and the X-15 aircraft went on to become one of the most successful flight research programs in the long history of the NACA and NASA.[22]

Although they failed to recognize such contributions, the Wiesner recommendations alerted NASA to the Kennedy administration's intentions. Despite the implications about his performance, Dryden remained publicly unaffected by the tempest, and the press left him unscathed. In the midst of the crisis, he managed to preserve a sense of calm and continuity at the agency. Dryden knew the criticism could only be answered by the new administrator; therefore, calling on reserves of patience and endurance, he concentrated on the tasks at hand and outlasted this painful episode.

His response reflected his view of life. In one of the many sermons he delivered from the Methodist pulpit, Dryden remarked that "one major mark of rank in the organic world is the capacity to suffer. The aim of life, therefore, is not to abolish suffering, for that would abolish sensitivity, but to eliminate its cruel, barbarous, and useless forms. To willingly accept toil, trouble, and suffering, these are goals for scientists as well as for other men."[23]

Worse suffering lay ahead. Later in the year a routine medical examination revealed a malignancy in his chest. After surgery and additional treatments, he returned not to reduced activity, but to the busiest schedule of his life. During the years remaining to him, the visits to the hospital recurred every few months, and the medications became more severe; yet the frantic pace of speeches, banquets, meetings, and professional conferences never slackened. Typically, he spoke of his affliction to no one.

In spite of the criticism and doubts raised by the Wiesner Report, the Deputy Administrator had long worked out for himself a clear and unchanging mental schematic of the nature of American space exploration. He divided it into three categories:

> The first includes those missions intended primarily to produce scientific data with respect to the space environment, the sun, earth, and planets and the galaxy, using telemetry of information from unmanned vehicles. The second is composed of earth satellite mis-

sions for application to meteorological research and weather forecasting, long distance wide-band communications, navigation, and similar tasks. The third relates to the travel of man himself in space, at first in a satellite orbit, later to the moon, and later to the planets and outer reaches of the solar system.[24]

Hugh Dryden devoted most of his waking hours to the achievement of the third segment of the U.S. space mission. He did so in tandem with President Kennedy's appointee as NASA Administrator, former Bureau of the Budget Director James E. Webb. Like Glennan, Webb agreed to the position only on condition of Dryden's continued service. So long in harness, Dryden acceded to the request.

Within three months of the Kennedy inaugural in January 1961, American human spaceflight received two powerful boosts—one from the successful orbital flight of Cosmonaut Yuri Gagarin, and another from the botched invasion of Cuba. The young President searched for ways to strengthen the image of his weakened administration and found his answer in space. The NASA Ten Year Plan had projected a lunar circumnavigation by astronauts. To defeat the Soviets at their game, especially after Gagarin's triumph, the U.S. required an even more daring enterprise. *Landing* astronauts on the Moon and returning them to Earth would assure an equal footing with the Russians. Both sides would have to start from the beginning, building all new spacecraft and boosters. On May 25, 1961, the President announced to a joint session of Congress his commitment to sending Americans to the lunar surface and back to Earth before the end of the decade.[25]

Dryden threw himself into the intricacies of human space flight with even greater enthusiasm than before. The conception and planning of Project Mercury bore his imprint from the very inception. Projects Gemini and Apollo also owed an immense debt to his heavy labors and quiet service. He found it possible to make such contributions because he and James Webb had established clearly defined spheres of operation. The administrator accepted as his highest priority to lobby and win the support of Washington's political elite for the space program as well as to convince the voting public of its value. The two men shared responsibility for the broad policy direction of the agency but to Dryden fell the hardest decisions involving technical and fiscal choices: which systems and subsystems to fund or to eliminate, to accept as presented or to modify; which scientific experiments to pursue; how to structure programs for maximum utility; how to obtain the cooperation of universities, corporations, and foreign powers; how to prepare and present budgets to congressional committees.

Dryden acted in this indispensable capacity not by attempting to superimpose his viewpoints on the NASA Headquarters and Center staffs. Instead, he served as Webb's savant, capable, as one historian has observed, of:

> solving the problems of Gordian knots without...

NASA executive meeting with left to right; Hugh L. Dryden, Deputy Administrator, James E. Webb, Administrator, and Dr. Robert C. Seamans, Jr. Associate Administrator. (NASA photo 66-H-93)

violently cutting through them. He did not cut through them, but neither did he neatly untie them. Instead, it was he who showed others how the untying was done—and without their ever being aware that they were under instruction. Dryden had a great talent for showing other brilliant men how to become even more brilliant, without their ever realizing how great had been his assistance. More often than not, Dryden's wisdom and judgment...were felt without ever being seen.[26]

While Dryden recognized the perils of defeat in the Cold War, he never regarded Projects Mercury, Gemini, and Apollo, the many unpiloted scientific probes, or the satellites launched during his tenure merely as demonstrations of American superiority. Rather, as he told Senator Robert S. Kerr (D, Oklahoma); Chairman of the Committee on Aeronautical and Space Sciences:

The setting of the difficult goal of landing a man on the moon and return to earth has the highly important role of accelerating the development of space science and technology, motivating the scientists and engineers who are engaged in this effort to move forward with urgency, and integrating their efforts in a way that cannot be accomplished by a disconnected series of research investigations in the several fields. It is important to realize, however, that the real values and purposes are not in the mere accomplishment of man setting foot on the moon, but rather in the great cooperative national effort in the development of science and technology which is stimulated by this goal....The national enterprise involved in the goal of manned lunar landing and return within the decade is an activity of critical impact on the future of this nation as an industrial and military power, and as a leader of the free world.[27]

Final Years

By 1965, the illness to which Dryden had given no quarter finally began to drain his capacity for resistance. He summoned his energy and flew to Hawaii to address a governors' conference, then stopped in Seattle to appear as keynote speaker at a meeting of the National Academy of Sciences. Upon returning to his desk in Washington, he resumed the customarily heavy schedule, then traveled again, once to New York and once to Chicago. On November 16, he entered the hospital for the usual periodic treatments, expecting to be released fairly soon, but his condition worsened, and he remained through Thanksgiving. Hugh L. Dryden died on the evening of Thursday, December 2, 1965. Despite the obvious physical decline, his degree of activity had long belied the true state of his health, and friends and colleagues expressed shock at his passing. President Lyndon Johnson, a great admirer of Dryden, whom he had known over a decade-long collaboration, told the nation that "no soldier ever performed his duty with more bravery and no statesman ever charted new courses with more dedication than Hugh Dryden. Whenever the first American space man sets foot on the moon or finds a new trail to a new star, he will know that Hugh Dryden was one of those who gave him knowledge and illumination."[28]

Dryden received many other accolades and awards during his lifetime and after his death, but perhaps his greatest and most appropriate honor came on March 26, 1976, when NASA renamed the NASA Flight Research Center as the NASA Hugh L. Dryden Flight Research Center. At the dedication ceremonies, then-NASA Administrator James C. Fletcher stated:

> in 1924, when the fastest racing planes did well to fly at 280 m.p.h, Dryden was already probing the transonic range of . . . flight. Later in the 1920s, he sought to develop methods of accurately measuring . . . turbulence in wind tunnels. In 1938, he was the first American to deliver the Wright Brothers Lecture at the Institute of Aeronautical Sciences. His "Turbulence and the Boundary Layer" became a classic summary of man's knowledge of the subject to date. It is most fitting that this Flight Research Center, with its unique and highly specialized capability for solving aerospace problems, should memorialize the genius of Hugh Dryden.[29]

NOTES

[1] Shirley Thomas, *Men of Space*, 8 Vols. (Philadelphia: Chilton, 1960-1968), II:65; Richard K. Smith, *The Hugh L. Dryden Papers, 1898-1965: A Preliminary Catalogue* (Baltimore: Johns Hopkins University, Milton S. Eisenhower Library, 1974), 19.

[2] Thomas, *Men of Space*, 65, 67; Smith, *Dryden Papers*, 19-20; Eugene M. Emme, "Astronautical Biography: Hugh Latimer Dryden, 1898-1965," *Journal of the Astronautical Sciences* (1977): 154; James H. Doolittle, "Hugh Latimer Dryden: A Tribute," reprinted from *Astronautics and Aeronautics* (1966): 1; Anon., "Dr. Hugh Latimer Dryden, 1898-1965," Headquarters National Aeronautics and Space Administration unpublished biographical sketch, December 2, 1965, 3, NASA Historical Reference Collection, NASA Headquarters, Washington, D.C.

[3] Raymond L. Bisplinghoff, "Hugh Latimer Dryden, 1898-1965," reprinted from *Applied Mechanics Reviews* (1966): 1; Thomas, *Men of Space*, 67; Smith, *Dryden Papers*, 19-20; Emme, "Astronautical Biography," 154.

[4] Emme, "Astronautical Biography," 154; Thomas, *Men of Space*, 68; Smith, *Dryden Papers*, 21.

[5] John T. Greenwood, ed., *Milestones of Aviation* (New York: Hugh Lauter Levin Associates, 1989), 97-98; Jerome C. Hunsaker and Robert C. Seamans, Jr., "Hugh Latimer Dryden, July 2, 1898-December 2, 1965," reprinted from *Biographical Memoirs of the National Academy of Sciences* (1969): 37-38; Smith, *Dryden Papers*, 22; Emme, "Astronautical Biography," 154-155; Bisplinghoff, "Hugh Latimer Dryden," 2; Thomas, *Men of Space*, 70.

[6] Smith, *Dryden Papers*, 23; Emme, "Astronautical Biography," 155-156; Hunsaker-Seamans, "Hugh Dryden," 39; Thomas, *Men of Space*, 69-70; Bisplinghoff, "Hugh Latimer Dryden," 2.

[7] Thomas, *Men of Space*, 72-73; Smith, Dryden Papers, 22; Hunsaker-Seamans, "Hugh Dryden," 40; Emme, "Astronautical Biography," 156.

[8] Smith, *Dryden Papers*, 23.

[9] Smith, *Dryden Papers*, 23; Emme, "Astronautical Biography," 156; Hunsaker-Seamans, "Hugh Dryden," 40; Thomas, *Men of Space*, 73-74.

[10] Michael H. Gorn, *The Universal Man: Theodore von Kármán's Life in Aeronautics* (Washington, D.C. and London: Smithsonian Institution Press, 1992), 98-117. For a reprint of *Where We Stand* and *Science, the Key to Air Supremacy* see Michael H. Gorn, ed., *Prophecy Fulfilled: Toward New Horizons and Its Legacy* (Washing-

ton, D.C.: Government Printing Office, 1994); "Dr. Hugh Dryden of NASA is Dead," *New York Times*, December 3. 1965.

[11] Bisplinghoff, "Hugh Latimer Dryden," 3; Smith, *Dryden Papers*, 24-25; Thomas, *Men of Space*," 76; Frank W. Anderson, *Orders of Magnitude: A History of NACA and NASA, 1915-1980* (Washington, D.C.: NASA SP-4403, 1981), 4.

[12] Roger E. Bilstein, *Orders of Magnitude: A History of the NACA and NASA, 1915-1990* (Washington, D.C.: NASA SP-4406, 1989), 24-26; Anderson, *Magnitude*, 2-12; Smith, *Dryden Papers*, 24-25; James R. Hansen, *Engineer in Charge: A History of the Langley Aeronautical Laboratory, 1917-1958* (Washington, D.C.: NASA SP-4305, 1987), passim.

[13] Quoted in Thomas, *Men of Space*, 77.

[14] Smith, *Dryden Papers*, 25; Emme, "Astronautical Biography," 159-160; Thomas, *Men of Space*, 77-78; Bisplinghoff, "Hugh Latimer Dryden," 3; Hunsaker-Seamans, "Hugh Dryden," 41-42; Bilstein, *Magnitude*, 44.

[15] Smith, *Dryden Papers*, 25-26; Thomas, *Men of Space*, 78-79; Emme, *Astronautical Biography*, 160; Anderson, *Magnitude*, 17.

[16] Emme, "Astronautical Biography," 160-163; Thomas, *Men of Space*, 78-79; Smith, *Dryden Papers*, 26; Bilstein, *Magnitude*, 47-48.

[17] Hunsaker-Seamans, "Hugh Dryden," 46.

[18] Bilstein, *Magnitude*, 48-49, 54, 56; Smith, *Dryden Papers*, 27; Thomas, Men of Space, 80; Emme, "Astronautical Biography," 164.

[19] Quoted in Thomas, *Men of Space*, 82; Smith, *Dryden Papers*, 28; Emme, "Astronautical Biography," 165; Bilstein, *Magnitude*, 63-64; Bisplinghoff, "Hugh Latimer Dryden," 4; Hunsaker-Seamans, "Hugh Dryden," 48. For an excellent, detailed account of Dryden's negotiations with Blagonravov, see Edward Clinton Ezell and Linda Newman Ezell, *The Partnership: A History of the Apollo-Soyuz Test Project* (Washington, D.C.: NASA SP-4209, 1978), 37-60.

[20] Bilstein, *Magnitude*, 49, 57; Emme, "Astronautical Biography," 165-167; Thomas, *Men of Space*, 81.

[21] James Schultz, *Winds of Change: Expanding the Frontiers of Flight, Langley Research Center's 75 Years of Accomplishment, 1917-1992* (Washington, D.C.: NASA NP-130, [1992]), 82-83; Richard P. Hallion, *On the Frontier: Flight Research at Dryden, 1946-1981* (Washington, D.C.: NASA SP-4303, 1984), 52, 323-326.

[22] Hallion, *On the Frontier*, 103-129; Wendell H. Stillwell, *X-15 Research Results* (Washington, D.C.: NASA SP-60, 1965), esp. 4, 6, 19, 26, 37, 45, 50-53, 56, 73.

[23] Emme, "Astronautical Biography," 166-168; Quoted in Hunsaker-Seamans, "Hugh Dryden", 49, and see 46-48; Smith, *Dryden Papers*, 27-29.

[24] Quoted in Thomas, *Men of Space*, 80; Emme, "Astronautical Biography," 168; Hunsaker-Seamans, "Hugh Dryden," 49; Smith, *Dryden Papers*, 29.

[25] Bilstein, *Magnitude*, 57-59; Anderson, *Magnitude*, 28.

[26] Smith, *Dryden Papers*, 28-29; NASA, unpublished biographical sketch, December 2, 1965, 11, seen in the Dryden File, NASA Historical Reference Collection.

[27] Quoted in Bisplinghoff, "Hugh Latimer Dryden," 4.

[28] Smith, *Dryden Papers*, 32; Quoted in Hunsaker-Seamans, "Hugh Dryden," 49.

[29] "Remarks by James C. Fletcher, Administrator, National Aeronautics and Space Administration, at the Dedication of the Hugh Dryden Flight Research Center, March 26, 1976," Fletcher Files, NASA Historical Reference Collection. Fletcher added that the Dryden Flight Research Center "was established in 1947—the same year Dr. Dryden became the NACA's second director. He played a key role in the aircraft tested here in its early years—the X-1, D-558, X-3, X-4, X-5, XB-70 and the X-15."

Key Documents

THE NATION'S MANNED SPACE FLIGHTS

by

Hugh L. Dryden
Deputy Administrator
National Aeronautics and Space Administration

(Address given before the Governor's Conference
on Oceanography and Astronautics, held at the
Kauai Surf Hotel, Lihue, Kauai, Hawaii,
October 1, 1965)

It has been an honor and a pleasure to accept the invitation of the Honorable John A. Burns, Governor of Hawaii, and the other officials of the State of Hawaii associated with him, to speak to the Governor's Conference on Oceanography and Astronautics. In reading the proceedings of the conference held in January of last year, I notice that the main focus of attention was the role of science and technology in the future of our nation, the nature of scientific and technological development, and the role of the State of Hawaii in contributing its part to the advancement of science and technology and their application to the problems of the modern world for the benefit of mankind. My talk deals with the newest of the frontiers of man, inaugurated on October 4, 1957, when man first left the surface of the earth to travel beyond the atmosphere in nearby space. I believe that Hawaii must participate in this enterprise for many reasons.

I recall a conversation during my visit to West Germany a few years ago for the purpose of exploring possible cooperation between the scientists and engineers of West Germany with the United States in the exploration of space, in accordance with one of the stated objectives of the National Aeronautics and Space Act of 1958, to conduct our activities in cooperation with other nations. My colleagues stated forcefully that Germany must find a way to participate in this enterprise if it ever hoped to become again a great leader in science and technology, for the exploration of space demands the most advanced developments in practically every field of science and technology to new levels of performance in every respect. An editorial in the New York Times of September 15, following a reference to some remarks by Mayor Willy Brandt of Berlin, stated that "businessmen and officials in many NATO countries share his (Brandt's) belief that the technological 'spin-off' from nuclear, missile and space research is giving American civilian industry a towering lead over its European competitors. It is certainly an exaggeration to say, as Mr. Brandt did, that West Germany will drop by 1975 to the status of a 'less-developed' nation unless it shares in American space-age know-how."

I do not believe that every country of the world must necessarily engage in the launching of satellites and space probes, although by means of bilateral, regional, and global agreement many nations can participate even in such activities. I believe that many nations can contribute through the use of sounding rockets and perhaps small earth satellites, and that opportunities can be made available for the scientists of the world to participate in both ground-based experiments essential to the space program and in the flight experiments.

Hawaii, of course, is one of our own fifty states and has already begun to make substantial contributions to our national program. I refer particularly to the Kokee Tracking Station in Kokee Park, which is one of the worldwide chain of stations for our manned space flight programs, and to our association with the University of Hawaii, looking to the expansion of astronomical facilities, particularly for more intensive observation of the planets on which we hope to land scientific instruments within the next few years, and to which, in the more distant future, we hope to send man himself. You are all familiar with the natural resources of Hawaii which make it most suitable for this purpose. I note also your association with the Communications Satellite Corporation, leading to an important role of Hawaii in the global communications via satellite.

But I believe that the interest of the citizens of Hawaii in space exploration and its importance to them lies not solely in the economic benefits that it may bring or in the material tools which it may contribute to our physical environment. Man is distinguished from other forms of life by his powers of reasoning and by his spiritual aspirations. Already the events of the last seven years have had a profound impact on all human affairs throughout the world. Repercussions have been felt in science, industry, education, government, law, ethics, and religion. No area of human activity or thought has escaped. The toys of our children, the ambitions of our young men and women, the fortunes of industrialists, the daily tasks of diplomats, the careers of military officers, the pronouncements of high church officials -- all have reflected the all-pervading influence of the beginning steps in space exploration. The impact can only be compared with those great developments of past history like the Copernican theory which placed the sun, rather than the earth, at the center of our solar system; the work of Sir Isaac Newton in relating the fall of an apple to the motion of the moon around the earth through the universal law of gravitation; to the industrial revolution; or other great landmarks in the history of mankind.

The origin of science can be traced far back in the distant past. Aristotle is quoted as saying that true science is the search of nature in the spirit of true scientific curiosity. For hundreds of years, science was mainly a purely intellectual activity, involving little of what we now call experimental science. Much has been written about those objectives of science which relate to gaining an understanding of the entire universe in which we live, of the excitement of studying the unknown, and of the contribution of science to man's intellectual and spiritual life. I wish to turn, however, to another aspect of scientific and technological development, which I may describe as the interaction of science, technology, and social need.

There is a mistaken impression in some circles today that scientific and technological development always proceeds by an orderly process in which, first, there is a basic concept or theory, followed by experimental verification, leading to further theoretical and experimental investigations and applied research, followed finally by application to some social need. Actually, of course, the situation is not so simple; the situation is a dynamic one with continual interactions between theory, experiment, application, and social need. In my reading of the history of scientific development, I have been impressed time and time again by the almost dominant role of the specific social environment in which the scientist and engineer work, which in most instances seems to be a prerequisite for the intensive development of the scientific concept itself as well as the ensuing technology. One or two examples will illustrate.

Most of the work for which Pasteur is famous originated in the social needs of the community in which he worked. Beginning in 1854 he addressed himself to the reason for unsatisfactory results obtained in the fermentation of beer, and in 1857 showed that the troubles arose from small organisms which interfered with the growth of yeast cells responsible for fermentation. Later he turned his attention to similar problems in the production of good wine. Later, under great social pressure, he studied the small organisms responsible for certain diseases of the silkworm, of cattle, of chickens, and of dogs and man. Thus social needs provided the incentive for and the support of Pasteur's scientific work in solving the "problems of the infinitely small."

Another classic story begins with the work of James Maxwell starting about 1850. In 1865 and 1873 he described the propagation of electromagnetic waves and suggested that light was a phenomenon produced by the travel of electromagnetic waves in the ether. I believe the first experimental demonstration of electric waves was by Hertz in 1883, who invented an oscillator to produce such waves. There was some limited further theoretical and experimental development by scientists such as Lodge and Righi in the last two decades of the nineteenth century. Marconi began a study of the application of electric waves to signaling in 1895 and succeeded in sending signals across the Atlantic in 1901. I think it is now obvious to everyone that this application by Marconi to a practical social need marked the beginning of greatly increased support for theoretical and experimental research in this field, that it marked the foundation of very large industrial developments, and that there has been a very great social impact.

These cases are of course the traditional ones that everyone quotes. There are many others, such as the development of probability theory and modern statistics from the "social need" of the members of high society in France interested in gambling.

I believe that in our world today social needs have become much more complex and go far beyond the material aspects of our life. A short time ago, at the bicentennial celebration of the Smithsonian Institution in Washington, the humanist Lewis Mumford attacked the notion that man is a creature whose use of tools played the largest formative part in his development. Said Mumford, "By what logic do we now take these tools away, so that he will become a functionless, workless being, conditioned to accept only what the Megamachine offers him: an automation within a larger system of automation, condemned to compulsory consumption, as he was once condemned to compulsory production. Instead of liberation from work being the chief contribution of mechanization and automation, I suggest that liberation for work, for educative mind-forming work, self-rewarding even on the lowest physiological level, may become the most salutary contribution of a life-centered technology."

I believe that activities in the exploration of space represent a "social need" in this broader sense. That it is a modern social need is recognizable from the passage of the National Aeronautics and Space Act and the appropriation of large sums of money by the Congress. This social need provides that essential environment to accelerate greatly the growth of theoretical and experimental science in many areas. It is true that this accelerated growth in science and technology is essential to the on-going development of space capability, but a deeper significance is the complex, dynamic interaction between science, technology, and space exploration, which is essential to the growth of science, technology, and space exploration. In this case, as in the cases previously cited, to use an analogy from bacteriology, there has to be a nutrient solution (money and employment opportunities) to feed the scientific and technological effort. And as soon as this environment is provided, many latent efforts in science and technology begin to assert themselves and move forward.

It is for reasons such as this that the citizens of our nation, including those of Hawaii, and in fact the citizens of the world, have a stake in the exploration of space.

The fundamental goals of our nation's space activities were expressed by Congress in the National Aeronautics and Space Act of 1958. The first of these is the expansion of human knowledge of the atmosphere and space, a goal which the President's Science Advisory Committee later restated as the "exploration of outer space in response to the compelling urge of man to explore and to discover." Prior to 1957, the exploration of outer space was carried on by astronomers in observatories on the ground, although some information about the lower atmosphere was obtained from sounding rockets, balloons, and airplanes. All of the information came to the astronomer in the form of waves radiated from the sun, the stars, and planets that reached our telescopes and spectrographs on the ground. Much of this radiation is blanketed out by the atmosphere, so that only a small fraction reaches the ground. However, during the past centuries, astronomers have learned a great deal about the composition of the stars, their life histories from the time of birth in the chance condensation out of the gas and dust of interstellar space, to their eventual destruction and the explosion of the supernovae.

Now the new tools of space exploration, the sounding rocket, the satellite, and the space probe, have made it possible to put instruments above the atmospheric curtain to cover the entire wavelength range from gamma rays to radio waves. Instruments can now be sent to the nearest planets, and probably in a few years to the outer reaches of the solar system. The knowledge obtained by these tools has come to be known as space science, but it is important to remember that this field is merely an extension of numerous scientific disciplines into the domain of space by means of the new tools.

Space science has already opened up completely new vistas on some of the oldest and most fundamental problems challenging science, including the structure of the universe, the abundance of the elements in the cosmos, the evolution of the stars and galaxies, the formation of the sun, and the origin of the earth. Extensive exploration has already been carried out in the near-earth region, the upper atmosphere, the ionosphere, and the magnetosphere in which the magnetic field lines anchored in the earth extend out into space. The investigations have been extended into the interplanetary medium beyond the influence of the earth's magnetic field. Finally, extensive attention has been given to the sun, whose activity is responsible for many of the phenomena observed in the space near the earth. Further, a beginning has been made on astronomical investigations made above the blanketing influence of the earth's atmosphere.

In the September issue of PHYSICS TODAY, Dr. Homer Newell reviews the impact of space techniques on geophysics. First, space techniques have provided new tools for studying old problems in such areas as geodesy, meteorology, upper atmospheric physics, ionospheric research, and sun-earth relationships. Second, space exploration has turned up a number of exciting new problems, greatly broadening the scope of the discipline. For example, the discovery of the Van Allen Radiation Belt on the flight of Explorer I led to the acceptance of a new concept, namely, that of the magnetosphere. It pointed to relationships among the solar wind, which was discovered by instruments in space probes, the magnetosphere, the radiation belts, the aurora, magnetic storms, ionospheric disturbances, and possibly even some influence of particle radiations on our weather.

Third, as space probes, and eventually men, reach other bodies of the solar system, such as the moon and planets, the domain of geophysics grows beyond the confines of a single body of the solar system and throws new light on the study of our own planet. Everyone is familiar with the vast amount of information obtained in three television transmissions, lasting less than 30 minutes each, from Rangers VII, VIII, and IX.

The instruments of these three spacecraft sent back a total of some 17,000 useful photographs of the lunar surface from altitudes ranging from more than 1000 miles in space down to virtually the point of impact. These photographs, by far the best ever taken of the moon, were so clear that astronomers can distinguish details as small as 18 inches across, with an accuracy 2000 times better than pictures taken from earth with conventional telescopes. The success of the Mariner IV flight to the planet Mars is well known. Philip H. Abelson, editor of the magazine SCIENCE, September issue, states that "the results of the Mariner IV mission constitute the most important advance in space research since the discovery of the Van Allen Radiation Belts." Photographs show that Mars resembles the moon in topography by exhibiting many craters but no evidence of mountain chains. The magnetic field of Mars is not more than 1/1000 that of the earth, and Mars has no radiation belt. One experiment gives independent evidence that the atmosphere of Mars is tenuous and unlike that of the earth.

The subject of this talk emphasizes the manned space flight program, so that further time cannot be given to the space science program in this talk. I do wish to remind you, however, that the scientific measurements of the space environment are absolutely essential in the design of satellites and space probes, whether manned or unmanned, in order to assure their successful operation in space. Thus Mariner IV, representing a superb engineering achievement, requiring the proper functioning of 134,000 parts after seven months in space, could not have been successfully designed to meet the rigors of the space environment without the advance knowledge provided by the scientific exploration of space.

As we pursue investigations in basic science in the space program, we are also developing areas of applications such as meteorology and communications. These, as much as anything else we do, will serve to knit closer together the peoples of this earth in a bond of better understanding of each other's problems and of mutual assistance and benefits that will come with better weather predictions. Nine Tiros meteorological satellites have been launched, as well as the first of the second-generation meteorological satellites, Nimbus I. Cloud pictures from these satellites are now being used daily by operational meteorologists in their weather predictions, as well as being used for research on the dynamics of the weather. Their role in the location and following of hurricanes has been well publicized. Equipment has been developed which automatically transmits the cloud pictures seen by Tiros to telemetry stations within range, so that any country is able to observe the local weather immediately on passage of the satellite.

Eight successful communication satellites have been launched of three types, namely: passive, two Echo spheres; low altitude active, including two Telstars and two Relays; and two synchronous satellites, Syncom II and III. These satellites have been used to demonstrate transcontinental and transoceanic communication in all its forms, including telephone, teletype, and television. The experimental work carried out by these satellites forms a foundation for the operational system now being established by the Communications Satellite Corporation in cooperation with many other nations. There are no real technical barriers to communication between individuals anywhere in the world, no matter how remote their locations. There are, however, many other problems, especially economic ones in providing the wider networks of ground communication from the individual to the transmitting and receiving terminals which are linked via the satellite. Certainly in the next decade international radio and television will be almost as commonplace as local broadcasts.

All of our flight missions are undergirded by a program of advanced research and technology, carried out in in-house government laboratories of NASA and other government agencies, and in industrial and university laboratories under contract. The work ranges from basic research to applied research and advanced technological development, and there are literally thousands of projects which cannot be described here in detail. The principal fields, all relevant to space exploration, are physical science, engineering science, cosmological science, socio-economic studies, vehicle systems technology, tracking and data acquisition and processing, space operations technology, space propulsion technology, flight medicine and biology, basic medical and behavioral sciences, and space biology (effects of space environment on biological phenomena and extraterrestrial life).

At present something more than half of our national space effort is devoted to manned space flight. Within the past three years we have made substantial progress in manned space flight in orbit about the earth. On February 22, 1962, John Glenn made three orbits in Friendship 7.

On May 24, the same year, Scott Carpenter made three orbits in Aurora 7. On October 3, Walter Schirra made six orbits in Sigma 7. And the program was completed with the flight of Gordon Cooper on May 15, 1963, in Faith 7, for 22 orbits. Project Mercury demonstrated that man can take his environment with him into space and there do useful work, for flight durations up to one day.

Attention was then turned to the Gemini program, and the first developmental flight took place on April 8, 1964, with the successful demonstration of the launch vehicle and guidance systems and of the structural integrity and compatibility of the spacecraft and launch vehicle. A second unmanned flight, Gemini 2, on January 19, 1965, utilized the Gemini capsule with all of its subsystems in a proof test. Then on March 23, the first manned flight, Gemini 3, was accomplished by Virgil Grissom and John Young, consisting of three orbits. On June 3, James McDivitt and Edward White traveled in Gemini 4 for 62 orbits. On one of these orbits, Edward White walked in space, and I will show you a color film of his walk at the end of this talk. On August 19, Gordon Cooper and Charles Conrad completed an eight-day mission in Gemini 5, which not only placed our country in first place for duration of mission but also broke several other records. The use of propulsion for maneuvering in space to change orbit was demonstrated, and certain experiments were made to study the problem of rendezvous with another spacecraft. Much more important, the Gemini 5 flight demonstrated that Project Apollo, which will send American explorers to the moon and back, is well within the physical capabilities of human astronauts. In the words of one of the engineers, this flight qualified the first subsystem of Project Apollo, i.e., the human crew, for the lunar mission.

The broad purpose of the Apollo program is the establishment of a national competence for manned space flight out to distances of the moon, including the industrial base, trained personnel, ground facilities, flight hardware, and operational experience. The use of this capability for manned flight to the moon and return and for further space explorations out to distances of the moon is intended to bring about United States leadership in space. We then will be in a position to do whatever our national interests require in the further study and use of this new environment.

The plan for reaching the moon in Project Apollo, as the culmination of our efforts during this decade to master the new environment of space, calls for sending three astronauts into orbit about the earth and then on a course toward the moon. Near the moon a rocket is fired to slow the Apollo spacecraft so that it goes into an orbit around the moon. Two astronauts then transfer to a moon ferry vehicle, fire a retro rocket, and descend to the lunar landing, using rocket thrust as a braking force since there is no atmosphere. The crewmen take turns leaving the ferry vehicle in their lunar space suits to explore the cratered surface of the moon.

Returning to the ferry vehicle, the two astronauts fire rockets that shoot them upward to rejoin the Apollo spacecraft and then head back toward earth and the tiny corridor about 40 miles high through which they can safely enter the atmosphere from space. Protected by a heat

15

shield, and in the later stages slowed by atmospheric drag and by parachutes, the astronauts return to earth.

To perform this mission, many capabilities must be developed and practiced, including the development of rockets capable of launching the required load to the moon, of making path corrections, of braking, and of taking off from the moon; the development of the technique of bringing two spacecraft together in space, which we call rendezvous; the development of the technique of physically joining them to become a single spacecraft, which we call docking; the development of capability of astronauts to operate outside the spacecraft in space; the development of maneuverable spacecraft; and the development of guidance and control for all phases of the mission including reentry. Some of these capabilities have already been demonstrated.

The development of rendezvous and docking begins with Project Gemini, the two-man spacecraft, which also permits an early test of the capabilities of men and machines up to periods of two weeks.

The Apollo three-man spacecraft will be fully exercised in earth orbit, practicing near the earth the rendezvous and docking maneuvers with the actual vehicles later to be used near the moon. It is estimated that NASA astroanuts will have accumulated at least 2000 hours of space flight time before we attempt the moon voyage.

The achievement of our space goals requires hard work, resourcefulness, and daring. It requires the skills and abilities of scientists, engineers, educators, industrialists, artisans, and craftsmen all over the Nation, and it requires the determination of the American people.

It is the aim of NASA to marshal a nationwide team of the most competent participants working toward a common goal in such manner as to strengthen our free institutions in industry, universities, government, and local communities.

We are carrying forward an active national space program, not limited to the moon, encompassing science, advanced engineering, and practical applications, including manned space flight.

We are building toward pre-eminence in every phase of space activity --all the way from microscopic electronic components to skyscraper-tall rockets.

We are building a network of large-scale engineering facilities, spaceyards, proving grounds, and spaceports to assemble, test, and launch the space vehicles we need now and in the future.

We are creating new national resources of lasting value in these facilities; in the industrial and managerial capabilities we are developing; and in the growing number of scientists and engineers who are learning about space and space technology.

We are filling the pipelines of hardware and knowledge, and, as measured by the financial resources required, were about halfway toward our first manned lunar mission in mid-1965.

We are accumulating, in space, the basic scientific knowledge about the earth, the solar system, the universe, and about man himself.

We are bringing benefits not only to the United States but to all the world through the use of space and space technology, employing such new tools as weather, communications, and navigational satellites, and

17

applying space-based techniques, equipment, and materials to improve industrial products, processes, and services.

We are providing a much-needed stimulus to the energies and creativity of people everywhere, particularly to the minds and aspirations of young people.

We are bringing about increased economic activity at a time when the effects of automation on our society are beginning to be felt.

And we are making certain, through our sustained efforts, that the realm of space now opening up to us shall be a domain of freedom.

It is for these reasons that we have mounted the greatest peacetime undertaking in the history of mankind.

Last year the German space pioneer Hermann Oberth quoted a word from his deceased colleague Eugen Sänger in a paper on "The Meaning of Space Travel" as follows: "Nature has placed a kindly veil over the goals which it has for us humans in her cosmic plan. In order to lead us to these goals, it has planted within us not only a bright intellect in the brain but also obscure impulses as a compass in our breasts. Eternal unrest and the will to go to far places for thousands of centuries let mankind wander over the entire earth. This eternal longing to wander let us develop land, sea, and air transportation. From the very beginning only the bare human instincts have determined the directions of human history until today and brought us to the threshold of space travel. Only the unclear distant travail of humanity will now lead us over this threshold. Space flight comes upon us as a natural event born in the deepest depths of the human soul, before which we can only stand humble or defiant; space travel comes upon us whether we love it or hate it or do not heed it at all, whether we believe in it or ridicule it, just as war and high flood tides and death come over us."

In a speech a few years ago, I gave my own answer to the question of the significance of space exploration to the ordinary citizen in every country of the world, as follows: "The exploration of space can give you new interests and new motivations arising from an expansion of your intellectual and spiritual horizons as you take a longer view of man's role in time and space at this point in the history of the human race."

President Johnson stated another goal in his remarks following the completion of the Gemini 5 mission. He said: "As man draws nearer the stars, why should he not also draw nearer to his neighbor?

"No national sovereignty rules in outer space. Those who venture there go as envoys of the entire human race. Their quest, therefore, must be for all mankind--and what they find should belong to all mankind."

The President has stated many times his hope that the exploration of space will draw mankind more closely together in friendship and cooperation. But seldom has he been more eloquent than in this statement, the closing words of which I would like to use at this time to conclude my own remarks:

". . . Gemini 5 was a journey of peace by men of peace. The successful conclusion is a notable moment for mankind--and a fitting opportunity for us to renew our pledge to continue our search for a world in which peace reigns and justice prevails . . .

"Gemini is but the beginning. We resolve to have many more such journeys--in space and on earth--until man at last is at peace with himself."

Thank you. And now let us view together some of the most dramatic moments in our manned space flight program: Astronaut Edward White's famous "walk in space."

...0...

MONICK/c

NEWS RELEASE
NATIONAL AERONAUTICS AND SPACE ADMINISTRATION
400 MARYLAND AVENUE, SW, WASHINGTON 25, D.C.
TELEPHONES: WORTH 2-4155 —— WORTH 3-1110

FOR RELEASE: IMMEDIATE
10:00 a.m., 25 March 1963

NEWS MEDIA BRIEFING

JOINT US-USSR TALKS
on
Cooperative Space Research Projects
Held in Rome, Italy

PARTICIPANTS:

DR. HUGH L. DRYDEN, Deputy Administrator, NASA.

MR. ALLAN J. FUNCH, Public Affairs Officer, NASA.

MR. FUNCH: Gentlemen, I think we shall proceed.

I am certain that you all know Dr. Hugh L. Dryden, Deputy Administrator of the National Aeronautics and Space Administration.

Dr. Dryden headed the United States delegation to the talks which were held in Rome with the delegation from the Soviet Union headed by Academician A. A. Blagonravov. These talks were designed to implement the agreement reached at Geneva last year and announced last December 5th at the United Nations.

Dr. Dryden will make some opening remarks, after which the session will be open to questions. Although this session has been termed a briefing, what is said here may be attributed to Dr. Dryden.

Gentlemen, Dr. Dryden.

DR. DRYDEN: Gentlemen, having survived a three-language press conference in Rome, with some confusion as to the product that came out, I thought I should make myself available to you to try to give an overall picture and perhaps a little of the atmosphere of what went on in Rome.

As was mentioned in the introduction, these meetings were to implement the agreement of Geneva. Those of you who may recall the terms of that agreement may remember that it was proposed that working groups be set up and that those working groups hold meetings in -- I have forgotten the exact dates -- at any rate, it has taken quite a while to arrange these meetings of working groups, but this is the nature of the Rome meeting, to implement the earlier agreement by talking about details.

The agreement itself provides for the usual sixty-day period during which both of us may change our minds on details and suggest changes. This gives an opportunity for review by various agencies within both governments, and changes can then be made without embarrassment. For that reason the text of the agreement will not be released until two months from March 20th, and I assume it will be released in the same way as the earlier one at the United Nations in New York. However, it is quite feasible to talk about the general subjects covered, although I will omit numerical data which are of interest to some of the technical journals.

The first subject treated was that of weather satellites, and the first section of the agreement deals with the matter of exchange of pictures and nephanalyses from satellites in both countries.

First of all, what kinds of pictures are to be exchanged. Not all of them, because the bulk would be so great, many are uninteresting. Therefore, the selection will be made, pictures of areas where there are no other weather observations, and pictures which show storm fronts, vortices, and so forth.

These selected pictures will be transmitted within a relatively small number of hours -- again I will omit the exact figure at this time -- in time enough to be of use in forecasting.

We talked about the method of indicating the location of the pictures, where were they taken, what part of the Earth, and the method selected and agreed to was that each picture would show latitude and longitude grids directly on the pictures which are transmitted, and accuracy figures were given for the accuracy of location.

We talked about the number of brightness levels, or what we in this country have usually called gray levels in the picture.

We talked about the field of view, how big an area on the surface of the Earth should be covered by the pictures.

It was agreed that nephanalyses, the cloud diagrams for all pictures, would be transmitted. Agreements were made about the scale, the kind of map projection that would be used. It was also agreed that conventional data which were of interest in the interpretation of satellite data would be transmitted as time was available on the communications link.

The next part of the weather satellite picture dealt with the communications link. If you recall the earlier agreement, it was provided that there would be a direct connection between Suitland, Maryland, and the Weather Forecasting Institute in Moscow. Because this word "communications" appears in the agreement in several senses there was some confusion at Rome. We are here talking about a hard-wire link by cable and hard line or microwave between these two centers. The specifications were spelled out. It was to be a four-wire full-time link capable of facsimile transmission, and the standards were described in terms of existing international standards. The nature of the terminal equipment was specified in detail, giving the drum speed and the other technical characteristics of the equipment.

The route of the line was determined. It was agreed that the testing of this line and installation of it would occur in early 1964.

It was agreed in principle that there would be an equal sharing of the costs, since it is of equal value to both countries. We had some discussion about business arrangements which have not yet been settled completely as to how this would be handled, but this will be settled probably before the two months are up.

We agreed that any country could have access to this communications link on a "receive only" basis, provided they are willing to pay a proper share of the cost, and so could have available for their use all information which passed over the link.

Finally, with respect to the satellites themselves, it has become I think clear that -- without talking about a specific number of satellites -- the objective is that each country maintain a working satellite continuously. If the life of the satellite is short, it will take a certain number. If it is longer it will take a smaller number. But the idea is that each of us should be able to take cloud observations, and that the meteorologists would coordinate the areas which are covered so as to get the maximum possible coverage of the Earth.

The agreement itself simply says that we will meet toward the end of this year to discuss the coordination of launchings.

If I may leave the subject of the agreement for a moment and just give you a little background, the Soviets said quite clearly that they were making tests of meteorological equipment in the present Cosmos series of satellites. It was also quite clear that, like ourselves, they are a little uncertain about launch times and slippages. While at various stages we had a little more refinement than to say that the Soviets expected to launch their satellites in

1964, when it came to the final text they did not want to be pinned down more closely than that. Actually, from some of the discussion it appears that they hope to be ready early in 1964, and I think this is indicated bo you by the desire that the communications link should be set up in the early months of 1964

To return to the text, the next section deals with experiments to be made with the next Echo satellite to be launched, the Echo II. The altitude of Echo II will not be sufficient for simultaneous visibility between the US and the USSR, and it is therefore necessary to use an intermediary. In the part of the agreement that is definite, this intermediary will be Jodrell Bank at the University of Manchester. The Russians will operate from their Zimenky Observatory, of Gorky State University.

QUESTION: Will you spell that, please?

DR. DRYDEN: Zimenky Observatory is Z-I-M-E-N-K-Y. The university is G-O-R-K-Y, Gorky State University.

QUESTION: Is that at Gorky?

DR. DRYDEN: Yes.

They are able to use 162 megacycles, which have been used from Jodrell Bank before, and is one of the frequencies that the Soviets have used in their satellite experiments.

The communication from here to Manchester will be by ordinary means -- cable or radio.

We ourselves are not so much interested in 162 megacycles because our chief interest in Echo II is in the rigidity and smoothness of the balloon. We really would like to use much higher frequencies, frequencies of the order of those we are using with the active communications satellites to get a finer resolution of detail.

We did get agreement that within the next few months the Soviets would consider the use of higher frequencies. This has to be considered jointly. It depends on the availability of equipment, of course, and the possibilities of modifying existing antennas.

If we use frequencies that are possible to be used from the Goonhilly Downs station, they may be an intermediate point in these experiments.

There is no money reimbursement in any of these projects. The Soviets have agreed to furnish tracking information of orbits over Russia that are not visible from the United States. They will carry out the usual types of communications experiments -- a carrier, single frequency modulation, telegraph, facsimile, and voice, if feasible.

As I mentioned before, departing from the text, in Rome, because of a conference in Russian, Italian and English, there was a lot of confusion between this communications experiment and the communication link that is used for the exchange of weather data. They are quite separate and have nothing to do with each other. We are not using Echo balloon to give weather data and so on.

The third area was that of magnetic field satellites. Here we ran into some difficulty and ran out of time, so that we will resume the discussions in Geneva at the time of the meeting of the Technical Subcommittee of the U.N. Committee on the Peaceful Use of Outer Space.

Let me emphasize again this is not a part of the U. N. meeting at all, but since many of our people will be at that meeting this will be a convenient time to continue the discussions. I think the matters at issue are not of great importance to you at this time. In general, we seek always to get close to the original data, the original observations themselves, and there is a little tendency to want to exchange data tha has various corrections made to it.

We were unable to resolve our different points of view at this time, and we will resume it in the future. So that present agreement contains only a paragraph stating that we have had useful discussions, that we have exchanged points of view, and that we are resuming discussions in May in Geneva. I had discussed privately with Blagonravov his willingness to have a meeting between scientists engaged in our Venus probe and the Russian scientists concerned with the Mars probe. We did, at the very end -- and this is the reason it was not in the press release itself, because it occurred really just before the final signing -- we got an agreement that scientists from these two projects would meet for discussions and exchanging of information at the time of the COSPAR meeting in Warsaw in early June. I think it is the first or second week in June.

Although not stated in the agreement, it was made clear that both sides would probably present formal papers at the COSPAR symposium, but what we are talking about here are the individual scientists getting together and talking in greater detail. That much is in the agreement and the press conference that was held in Rome. In reporting this, I expressed the hope that this would ultimately lead to the coordination of experiments or interplanetary probes since certainly there is no secrecy as to the launch date. Everybody knows when they will be launched.

mcc-2

It would seem that we could both get better coverage if we used somewhat different instrumentation in many cases and agreed to exchange the results. I do not know that this meeting of scientists will lead immediately to that, but I think in future discussions with the Soviets it is possible that agreements of this kind would be reached. Blagonravov was asked his views on the future cooperative areas and mentioned particularly the area of space science, the information necessary for man's exploration of the universe. So much for the content of the agreement.

I thought you might be interested in a little background kind of information. I understand a Newsweek fellow got some of it out of the Russian correspondents, so I had better give you this story. All three of our meetings have had a kind of protocol that we would meet first in the territory of one and then in the territory of the other, so that in this case, the first meeting -- actually there was a ceremonial of sorts, a greeting of the two delegations by the counselor of the U. S. Embassy in the absence of the American Ambassador in the Ambassador's Office. The counselor's name, I believe, is Williamson.

There was no room in the Embassy itself, so that we met in an office building at 25 Via Abruzzi, which is the new offices of the Veterans Administration in Rome. I didn't know that the Veterans had an office in Rome, but it is the central point for all of Europe, and the director was to move into his office last week. He postponed his moving in for a few days to give us a chance to use those rooms.

The second meeting, since we had met in the U. S. Embassy and been greeted by the Ambassador, it was necessary that we go to the U.S.S.R. Embassy and be greeted by the Soviet Ambassador. This was done and the second meeting continued at that location. Following then, we alternated between Via Abruzzi and, not the Soviet Embassy, but the summer home of the Ambassador, which is outside the walls of Rome, a very magnificent villa with Gubelin tapestries and sculpture and one thing and another.

Actually, Blagonravov and his wife and one or two others were living on the upper floors of this summer residence. The Ambassador was not in residence there. Generally the pattern was to meet in the morning for about three hours, 9:30 to 12:30, meeting separately in the afternoon from about 2:30 to 6. After you got established you came in with a draft from the day before on both sides and compared points and argued matters of substance and wording. So this continued throughout the period. Roughly there were 24 hours of joint meetings spread out over about eight days. In addition, there were some individual discussions as people met on sight-seeing tours or at the meetings of the IQSY this last week. There was very little in the way of fraternizing socially, so to speak. There were two social occasions, a cocktail party given by Ramberg, the Science Attache of the U. S. Embassy at his residence, and a cocktail party given by the Soviets in the Russian Embassy.

After the signing, and while we were waiting for the cars from the Embassy to come out to the summer residence of the Ambassador, the Russians brought out caviar and vodka to properly celebrate the occasion. I mention that because I know that one paper has the story, a magazine, and will probably use it. I will not defend my reputation for not drinking vodka, but obviously there was some pressure on the part of the Russians and ourselves in having come out with something definite.

There was no atmosphere of cold war anywhere, and has not been in these meetings since the first one in New York when Blagonravov read the Russian protest against the nuclear tests in the atmosphere, at which time he finished the reading by saying that he did this on request -- by direction. Since that time, after we made it clear we had no instructions in that area, had no competence in that area and would not engage in this type of discussion, there has never been a mention of any of these questions which have been agitated so much by the Soviet political group in other quarters.

There was, so far as we can tell, only one political or semi-political person in the group. I think you have the list -- it was Mr. Stacheffski, of the Foreign Office. In our early meetings he had tried to exercise a little control over the Soviet delegation, for example, in the matter of whether to sign a piece of paper or not. He had been overruled by Blagonravov. It has been clear ever since that Blagonravov is in charge of the delegation.

The general atmosphere has been a friendly one. There is an evident desire to cooperate within the political framework of both countries. It has been realized on both sides that the only hope at the present time is to stay in areas that are not at the apex of the cold war. There were two Russian women present -- Mrs. Blagonravov and Blagonravov's secretary. They were the only women in the Soviet delegation.

There was a little friendly barter and gifts made. I noticed some of our people exchanging Tiros cuff links or tie clasps or other little articles for similar Vostok items.

mcc-4   Mr. Klokov of the Communications Ministry, had a supply of recent Russian stamps, including all of the austronauts and the celebrations connected with aviation and so forth. Mrs. Blagonravov had given presents to the wives of a few of us, and we naturally responded in kind.

I have the feeling that this simply illustrates the fact that Russia is a very large nation, that there are very many groups within it with different ideas and different proposals, and that in this case here is a group of scientists who wish to engage in cooperation.

This is a very long statement. Just one more aspect that has interested some people. These are the difficulties connected with language. There were quite a battery of translators present on both sides, but we have found repeatedly that the mere traslation of a word from one language to a word in another language is not sufficient to convey the meaning, that there are all sorts of connotations that have to be taken into account.

One instance, we used the phrase of exchanging things of interest and value. In Russian they did not know how to translate this. In Russian the two words are essentially the same. And I guess we rationalize it by saying that the Russians aren't interested in anything that doesn't have value. At any rate, here is a shade of meaning that they don't seem to have. They had trouble with English words. Very often the English text was not changed, but there had to be a few more words in the Russian language.

For example, we gave a different accuracy for the pictures on which landmarks were available. This English word "landmarks" gave them somewhat of a problem. Apparently, there is no Russian word which says exactly the same thing. We talk about the gray levels of the picture, and that, of course, is a kind of slang. It was finally changed to brightness level to correspond with the word which meant more to the Russians.

We talked about making results available to the scientific and technical community. The use of the word "community" in that sense is peculiar to the English language, apparently, so they stated it in terms of making it available to scientists and technical people, or something of that sort. But I think the one perhaps which is more striking, we had used the language of the Echo experiment. We said, I guess, the "Echo satellite be used for a program to demonstrate communications between the U.S. and U.S.S.R." They could not accept this. It took us a very long time to find out what the trouble was. It turned out the trouble was with the word "demonstrate." A demonstration in the continent is a group of miners marching on Paris, or it is a political demonstration of some sort. They thought we had introduced this word to indicate that we were going to have Mr. Kennedy call Mr. Khrushchev, or make some kind of political hay out of this.

The whole difficulty disappeared by simply phrasing it that we would make an experiment to test the feasibility of direct communications. This will give you a little idea of some of the problems that come up. It doesn't pay to be suspicious too early. You have to explore by asking the same questions many different ways in order to discover what the meaning is.

Many of you have heard stories of other international conferences where something spoken has aroused fury and resentment, and afterwards it was found merely the choice of word by a translator had given an erroneous impression. So that we wonder what we did for 24 hours. It is a tedious job in many ways, not as direct and straightforward as you might think. I think that is all I have to say.

QUESTION: Dr. Dryden, when you say the matter of hours would intervene in the selection of the pictures and so forth, and then it would be communicated on the communications link, in time for forecast, do you mean for that same day?

DR. DRYDEN: Yes, that's right. I don't want to state the figure because there might be some negotiation to change it.

QUESTION: Dr. Dryden, you have emphasized in the past that this must be a two-way exchange.

DR. DRYDEN: Yes.

QUESTION: Is all of this cooperation in the weather satellite conditional upon their launching of the weather satellite?

DR. DRYDEN: We have made it very clear that the purpose was to exchange satellite data. We have essentially written in restrictions on the use of the line for ordinary meteorological data only if time remains after the other pictures are transmitted. We have also made it clear that while we will not count picture for picture, that there must be a substanially equivalent flow both ways, that the line will really not be activated until such exchange is available.

We are in the position, of course, at any time to stop transmitting over the direct line if we are not satisfied with the performance on the other side.

In addition, since pictures of course degrade on transmission over such a line, it has been agreed that pictures will be mailed, that is, some of the original pictures will be mailed so that we can assess the quality of the transmission.

There is provision made that on nephanalyses, which have to be transmitted for all pictures, that if there is an interesting area we can ask for the picture for that area, and they can do the same.

QUESTION: Why, on this communications link, did you decide to set up a direct bilateral rather than working through the WMO?

DR. DRYDEN: The reason of course is that we are the two satellite launching countries. It has been agreed from the beginning that we would permit these drop-offs if there were pro rata sharing of the cost. There are no direct links now

rjm 2   13

which permit facsimile transmission to the Soviet Union.

There is a general paragraph in the introduction that the summation must conform to the recommendations of the WMO. There is no attempt to evade the WMO in this proceeding at all. In fact, it is to supply the information for the WMO countries.

QUESTION: But any countries can just tap the wire, so to speak, if they paid the freight; is that it?

DR. DRYDEN: Yes, that is right.

QUESTION: Does this apply to Communist China or only UN members?

DR. DRYDEN: Oh, no. This line doesn't go anywhere near Communist China.

QUESTION: Could you tell us the route, Dr. Dryden?

DR. DRYDEN: Generally across Europe. Again I don't want to specify in detail.

QUESTION: How long is this weather satellite agreement to last?

DR. DRYDEN: It is an open agreement. There is no time limit.

QUESTION: You pointed out that each country has agreed to have a functioning satellite up at all times. And you said that would depend of course on the life of the satellite. How can you make such determination without some idea of what the life of the experiment is in the agreement?

DR. DRYDEN: The fact is that this country will maintain a weather satellite up at all times. In fact, perhaps more than one, before we get through. So we are not making any commitment that is piled on top of an existing commitment.

QUESTION: Is our participation in this program based on the Nimbus satellite or the Tiros satellite?

DR. DRYDEN: Well, from their own statement, 1964 is the year when they will be ready. We hope the Nimbus will be ready at that time.

QUESTION: Then why is bilateral -- why is the bilateral experiment necessary if we are going to get 100 percent coverage

rjm 3   14

with the Nimbus anyway, aren't we?

      DR. DRYDEN: Not quite. But approaching it. Here again, one Nimbus goes over a certain place on the Earth once per day -- one time. If you want the weather at noon everywhere, you wouldn't get it with one satellite.

      The coordination means that the Russian satellite would be launched at such a time that we would get greater coverage in time.

      QUESTION: Then there would actually be coordination as to the time of launch?

      DR. DRYDEN: That is correct, yes.

      QUESTION: Dr. Dryden, getting back to this direct communications link, how many teletype channels would be available here?

      DR. DRYDEN: Just one each way. It is a four-line circuit.

      QUESTION: This means that you can carry facsimile plus one two-way teletype?

      DR. DRYDEN: No. There will be a facsimile, we hope, flowing both ways all the time, or nearly all the time.

      QUESTION: What I am trying to get at, perhaps indirectly have we established this direct communications link between the Kremlin and the White House, which has been discussed ever since the Cuban crisis?

      DR. DRYDEN: We have established a facsimile connection between Suitland, Maryland and some location that I don't know exactly, in Moscow. We specified that this link is to be used for meteorological purposes. I think there is some fear on the Russian side that we might want to use this for political purposes. The intention is that this is not the direct link that has been talked about. And of course it is fairly simple to set up a channel, a telephone channel, if you want a telephone channel, or teletype channel, to Moscow. You people do it every day in your business. Why should they bother this link with that kind of traffic?

      QUESTION: What would be the mechanism, sir, to use

Jodrell Bank as an intermediary on the Echo experiments?

DR. DRYDEN: The mechanism is that we agree that we would arrange that, and we have already had discussions with the British authorities and with Lovell.

QUESTION: How will it work? Lovell will make the observations for us?

DR. DRYDEN: No, no. We will have a cable or radio link to him so that we can, ourselves, receive information via the satellite, as well as receiving it in Jodrell Bank.

QUESTION: Dr. Dryden, in the early agreement -- I think the document we got last December -- it spoke about two phases of this thing.

DR. DRYDEN: That's right.

QUESTION: In the experimental stage each country would put up one satellite. Then after that the thing would become an operational thing and transmission would be made in real time.

DR. DRYDEN: Yes.

QUESTION: Does that mean hot off the satellite without any selection of pictures or anything like that?

DR. DRYDEN: No. There is no provision for read-out of each other's satellites, if this is what you are driving at. The satellite information would be received in Moscow, the pictures selected and transmitted, but within a relatively few hours of the actual observation. You see up to an hour or hour and a half would be taken up in the satellite coming around over its read-out station. Then there would be the time necessary to look at the pictures and make a selection. There will be time required to put the grid on it, which locates it. But all of this can be done within a relatively small number of hours.

QUESTION: It would be quicker than during the experimental phase, is that the point?

DR. DRYDEN: Well, --

QUESTION: Transmission from --

DR. DRYDEN: Essentially the experimental phase is simply experiments made nationally without the exchange of pictures. What this amounts to is the Soviets will be ready to exchange pictures sometime in 1964.

QUESTION: How long does it take the Tiros station to process its pictures and make a nephanalysis which is of value, say, to transatlantic jet pilots, as we are doing now?

DR. DRYDEN: I don't know what the record is. It is certainly within six hours.

QUESTION: Within six hours?

DR. DRYDEN: Yes.

QUESTION: Would it be expected then that a figure like six hours would be shot for in this thing?

DR. DRYDEN: This is not the exact number, and I say I don't want to give you the exact number until the 60-day period is up. It is of that order of magnitude.

QUESTION: That is what I meant.

DR. DRYDEN: It is not 24 hours, it is not 12 hours. It doesn't happen to be six. But --

QUESTION: Is there any question of the necessity of compatibility of equipment here? Does their equipment have to be the same as ours so that at some time in the future we might be able to tap?

DR. DRYDEN: No. It is quite clear the compatibility is in the product, the picture. Nothing is said about the nature of the apparatus which gives you that picture.

QUESTION: Dr. Dryden, I wonder if you could elaborate a little bit for us on the nature of the experiments that the Soviet Union has already done in weather satellites. Have they been taking pictures?

DR. DRYDEN: They did not tell us. They did not tell us. They simply said that they are making experiments with the Cosmos series.

QUESTION: They didn't tell us whether they have been

taking pictures of cloud cover of the United States, for example?

       DR. DRYDEN: The inference was that they had been taking pictures of cloud cover. I don't know where.

       QUESTION: Dr. Dryden, on the basis of your talks in Rome, do you feel that the Soviets are sufficiently advanced in weather satellites to be an equal partner with us in this whole business.

       DR. DRYDEN: I think it is obvious that they are not right at this moment but that they hope to be in 1964.

QUESTION: Dr. Dryden, up on the Hill the question is being raised as to why we should cooperate with the Soviet Union in these two areas of communications and weather, since these are areas that are also of great interest to the military. I wonder what your answer is to this kind of objection?

DR. DRYDEN: The weather, I think, ordinarily is regarded as not specifically a military topic. The military is interested in certain detailed aspects of weather in connection with their operations. The satellites, more specifically, give you global weather. You cover a substantial area with cloud pictures, several hundred miles on a side. In general the military interest perhaps is in smaller areas.

I would say that just as in communications, ordinary carriers satisfy a very large fraction of the needs of the military. They rent channels just as you do. There are some areas of military communications that are not satisfied by commercial carriers. I think all I would say is that the Nimbus system has worked out to cover the general military requirements for weather data. There may be special requirements not covered.

QUESTION: On this Echo satellite, would you elaborate just a little about how this will work? Do we understand that when the satellite is mutually visible to the United States and Jodrell Bank, the signal would be sent through space?

DR. DRYDEN: No.

QUESTION: How does that work?

DR. DRYDEN: This is not the present plan. The present plan is when it is mutually visible from Jodrell Bank and Russia that we will talk via cable or radio to Jodrell Bank, which will then transmit it via satellite to Russia.

QUESTION: But there would be no European land lines and space link across the Atlantic?

DR. DRYDEN: No. We have done enough experimenting of that kind, I think.

QUESTION: Dr. Dryden, what areas would we like

coverage with a Russian weather satellite in terms of our Nimbus system? Are there some geographical --

DR. DRYDEN: The areas of most concern to the worldwide weather people are the very large ocean areas where there are very few observations of any kind, and the weakest areas are those in the Southern Hemisphere, of course.

QUESTION: Dr. Dryden, is there anything in the event of another crisis, like the Cuban crisis, to prevent use of this link between the United States and Russia to prevent communications between the leaders --

DR. DRYDEN: This is a hypothetical question. I guess Khrushchev still runs the Soviet Union and Mr. Kennedy has pretty much of a voice on this side.

There is no necessity that this link be used. If the White House wants a link to Russia, they can set it up in, I would guess, about half an hour, through the ordinary channels.

QUESTION: Dr. Dryden, was there any discussion of the possibility of exchange of scientists so that --

DR. DRYDEN: No.

QUESTION: -- selection of pictures could be made at the point they are received before --

DR. DRYDEN: Not at the present time. This is one matter that is not directly covered. Frankly, we hope that we can lead into this kind of a situation. But at the present time the whole matter of rockets, space vehicles, space technology, in Russia is completely classified. And if you are going to base agreement on breaking that wide open at the present time, then we have no kind of agreement.

QUESTION: I was speaking in this case of only the picture product to make the decision on what is to be transmitted back.

DR. DRYDEN: At the present this does not provide for this kind of exchange of personnel. It does provide for the possibilities of the meteorologists at the two ends to interrupt the facsimile and talk by telephone directly.

QUESTION: Was there any discussion at all between you and Blagonravov or any of your other people about the possibility of joint launchings? You say that it is completely classified; we understand that.

DR. DRYDEN: We started this in the early days. It was quite obvious that they would not consider that, and that they would not consider read-out by others.

QUESTION: So in this 24-hour period of talks this wasn't even brought up?

DR. DRYDEN: This wasn't brought up.

QUESTION: Dr. Dryden, you mentioned that they would provide tracking information over the Soviet Union.

DR. DRYDEN: Yes.

QUESTION: This is the first time, as far as I can recall, in which they will provide tracking information of our satellites. Is this restricted to Echo II?

DR. DRYDEN: This, at the moment, is restricted to the Echo.

QUESTION: Was there any discussion --

DR. DRYDEN: There is no adjective in front of it. It might be optical tracking.

QUESTION: Was there anything opening the door to cooperative tracking of satellites?

DR. DRYDEN: Cooperative tracking? They are willing to consider the question of radar tracking, but they cannot -- they could not make this commitment because obviously the radar is the property of the military. But they are going to take up the question particularly in the inflation period of Echo of making radar observations.

QUESTION: And then reporting them to us?

DR. DRYDEN: Yes.

QUESTION: By what means; did they say?

DR. DRYDEN: Since at the moment it is a fact that they will consider, this is again one of those things which may change within the sixty days. I perhaps am going too far even in making a point of this.

QUESTION: Why would tracking of a satellite over the Soviet Union be of any particular interest to us if we know the orbit?

DR. DRYDEN: Only in the question of up-dating. The particular interest actually as I have indicated is during the inflation period. This is the main interest.

QUESTION: Dr. Dryden, if the Russians really wanted to have a direct read-out of our Nimbus weather satellite, couldn't they buy cheap equipment?

DR. DRYDEN: They wouldn't need to buy it. They could probably make it without any problem. This becomes a matter of national policy.

The intention, of course, is to broadcast continuously, although I must remind you that that is under our control. This is one of the things which can be commanded on or off in the satellite.

We have not given consideration of any attempt to deny this to the Russians. We would be denying ourselves and denying other countries nearby.

VOICE: Thank you very much, Dr. Dryden.

(Whereupon, at 10:50 a.m., the briefing was concluded.)

NATIONAL AERONAUTICS AND SPACE ADMINISTRATION
WASHINGTON 25, D. C.

The Honorable Robert S. Kerr   June 22, 1961
Chairman, Senate Committee on
  Aeronautical and Space Sciences

My dear Senator Kerr,

    As you suggested during my recent discussion before the Committee, I will attempt to put in writing the remarks I made as to the significance of the program recommended by the President for landing a man on the moon and his safe return by the end of the decade to the present and future welfare of this nation.

    The attainment of the goal stated by the President requires extensive research and development in almost every branch of science and technology at the frontiers of knowledge in these various fields. New materials and components must be developed to function in the extreme cold and the extremely low pressures of outer space, at the extreme speeds, and at the extreme temperatures attained in rocket combustion chambers and on the outer surface of bodies reentering the atmosphere at high speed. New developments in propulsion, in electronics, in communications, in guidance and control techniques, in computer techniques, are necessary in order to accomplish the task. New information in the life sciences, including the effects of the radiations encountered in outer space, the effects of long periods of weightlessness, and long exposure to a completely closed environment--all these are required and will provide new basic information about the performance of the human body under adverse conditions. This new knowledge and experience in the space sciences and technologies will provide the sound basis for applying our new-found knowledge to the design of space vehicles for a variety of purposes, some now foreseen, others unthought of at present. These applications include not only space vehicles for scientific research, for communications systems, for meteorological observation, and presently unforeseen civil uses, but also space vehicles for potential applications in the national defense. Space technology, like aeronautical technology, can be applied to military systems, and we must be well advanced in this technology to avoid its possible exploitation against us.

    Equally important is the fact that these developments in science and technology are transferable to other applications in our industrial society. We have had repeated evidence in the history of the development of the automobile, the airplane, and the nuclear reactor of the transferability of developments in these fields to other industrial applications. The development of space science and technologies strengthens our whole industrial base and serves as insurance against technological obsolescence. Education will profit. The discipline of cooperation in a great national effort may well be the instrument of great social gain. Many hope that space may be an area where all the nations of the world may learn to work together for the benefit of all men.

The setting of the difficult goal of landing a man on the moon and return to earth has the highly important role of accelerating the development of space science and technology, motivating the scientists and engineers who are engaged in this effort to move forward with urgency, and integrating their efforts in a way that cannot be accomplished by a disconnected series of research investigations in the several fields. It is important to realize, however, that the real values and purposes are not in the mere accomplishment of man setting foot on the moon but rather in the great cooperative national effort in the development of science and technology which is stimulated by this goal.

The billions of dollars requred in this effort are not spent on the moon; they are spent in the factories, workshops, and laboratories of our people for salaries, for new materials, and supplies, which in turn represent income to others. It is unfortunate that space exploration is still so new that journeys of man to the moon are synonymous with foolish or visionary enterprises as described in science fiction. Fifty years ago flying through the air had the same connotations--risky, expensive, useful only as a sport. Our lack of appreciation of the potentialities of aeronautics extended through the early years, forcing the Wright Brothers to go abroad. We entered the first World War with no design capability and no manufacturing experience, dependent completely on foreign designs. Only after the war did we begin to devote effort to research in the new aeronautical technology. We must not undergo the same experience in space science and technology. The national enterprise involved in the goal of manned lunar landing and return within the decade is an activity of critical impact on the future of this nation as an industrial and military power, and as a leader of a free world.

/s/ Hugh L. Dryden
Deputy Administrator

A National Space Program for the United States

by
Dr. Hugh L. Dryden, Director
National Advisory Committee for Aeronautics

for presentation at the
Tenth Annual California Wing Convention
Los Angeles, California
April 26, 1958

My first airplane ride was in a Curtiss Eagle. It was one of the first of America's first trimotors, powered by Curtiss engines rated at 150 horsepower each. The brochure -- I still have it -- described the airplane as an "aerial limousine, with plywood cabin giving full protection from wind, and reduction of noise so as to permit conversation." Top speed was a little more than 100 mph and cruise was hardly 80mph. Nothing was said about range.

The Curtiss Eagle was obviously the ultimate in air transport. The brochure strongly suggested that thought. I was in no mood to challenge the obvious, because that was in 1919 and I had yet to learn how quickly and surely "ultimate" achievements in aeronautics are surpassed.

I must confess that in 1919, if anyone had predicted that 40 years later, commercial transport across country would be scheduled at 550 mph, well, I would have been skeptical. My inclination today, based on the

- 2 -

rapidity of yesterday's progress, is not to say things can't or won't happen. Besides, it has been far more satisfying to have been involved in some of the work that contributes to our progress in the realm of flight.

On April 2, President Eisenhower sent a message to the Congress, recommending that aeronautical and space science activities sponsored by the United States be conducted under the direction of a civilian agency, except for those projects primarily associated with military requirements. The draft legislation, sent to the Hill at the same time, centers responsibility for administration of the civilian space science and exploration within a new National Aeronautics and Space Agency, the nucleus of which will be the National Advisory Committee for Aeronautics.

The President has directed NACA to prepare the specific new space programs that NASA should undertake. He has also instructed NACA to present to the appropriate committees of the Congress a full explanation of the proposed legislation and its objectives.

These facts will explain why I am here today to discuss with you, in even the necessarily broad terms I shall use, "A National Space Program for the U.S.."

The need for the United States to assert its leadership in the fields of space technology is self-evident. For the record, however, I

- 3 -

should like to note the four reasons the President's Science Advisory Committee has listed as giving urgency and immediacy to our advancement in space technology. They are: (1) the compelling urge of man to explore the unknown; (2) the need to assure that full advantage is taken of the military potential of space; (3) the effect on national prestige of accomplishment in space science and exploration; and (4) the opportunities for scientific observation and experimentation that will add to our knowledge of the earth, the solar system, and the universe.

The space programs that must be promptly undertaken and vigorously carried to completion fall into three groups. First, there are projects for development of satellites and space craft such as those used for reconnaissance. These, clearly, are activities that are, and I quote from the language of the proposed legislation, "peculiar to or primarily associated with weapons systems or military operations." Such projects would be carried forward by the Department of Defense. Then, there are projects for development of satellites and space vehicles with the special capabilities required by the scientific community to probe the secrets of our solar system. Projects in this second category would be the responsibility of NASA. Finally, there are space projects that will be useful for both military operations and the data-gathering needs of civilian science.

Space projects in this third project will be reviewed jointly by the Department of Defense and the NASA to determine where responsibility shall be lodged or whether the projects will be undertaken cooperatively. I, for one, might be concerned about the difficulties that could be expected to arise in these negotiations, were it not that since 1915 the military services and the NACA have worked together -- closely and harmoniously. The fact that we are moving into the new, unexplored areas of space merely increases the essentiality of this effective partnership.

Since the President's message on space, we have conferred frequently with responsible officials of the Department of Defense -- among them, the Deputy Secretary of Defense, Donald A. Quarles; ARPA Director, Roy W. Johnson, and ARPA, Chief Scientist, Herbert York. On both sides there has been evident a firm resolution that the military and civil segments of our space program be so administered that taken together they are of maximum benefit to our country.

As our exploration of space proceeds, I expect we shall find that most of the progress made in the technology will be applicable to satellites and space craft whether they are operated for military or civil purposes. My confidence on this point is based on the knowledge that in aeronautics, the research advances made in aerodynamics, propulsion and structures have been promptly used, first by the designers of military airplanes and then by the builders of commercial aircraft. The research and development performed under military auspices will be valuable in furthering our space exploration for civilian purposes. The flow of useful information in the opposite direction will be similarly beneficial.

Over the past 43 years, the research activity of the NACA has been directed toward solution of the problems of flight. Until the end of World War II, these programs were focused mainly on problems peculiar to airplanes. Since then, we have been working increasingly to provide information useful in the design of missiles. Today, more than 50 percent of the effort of our 8,000 scientists, engineers and supporting personnel is applicable to missiles, satellites and space craft.

As stipulated in the draft legislation, the NASA will, and I quote, "plan, direct, and conduct scientific studies and investigations of the problems of manned or unmanned flight within or outside the earth's atmosphere with a view to their practical solution." Beyond this responsibility, study of the problems of flight, the bill provides that NASA shall develop, test, launch, and operate aeronautical and space vehicles, and that it shall arrange for participation by the scientific community in the planning of scientific measurements and observations to be made through use of aeronautical and space vehicles; and conduct or arrange for the conducting of such measurements and observations; and provide as appropriate for dissemination of the data collected.

The first of these new responsibilities over and beyond today's functions of NACA -- the development, testing, launching and operation of aeronautical and space vehicles -- I wish to discuss in more detail a little latter. Respecting the second, it is imperative that the best scientific judgement available be employed to determine our space science objectives, and to this end it will be necessary that NASA work most closely with the National Science Foundation and our National Academy of Sciences. Again, as instructed by the President, we have already begun discussions with these bodies, as well as other governmental and non-govermental bodies to insure participation by the scientific community in the planning and coordination of the scientific programs for the use of space vehicles in civilian science.

Much has been said in recent months about these civilian science programs. I should like now to quote several scientists about the kind of fundamental, new information in their specialties that use of space vehicles can be expected to provide. This type of information, I might add, can be obtained only from positions out in space.

First, the statement of a geophysicist: "Observations of the man-made satellites will lead to important conclusions as to the precise shape of our planet. The plotting of the trajectories of a number of artificial satellites will finally enable us to determine the exact configuration of the earth, an extremely important element in the study of the origin, history and structure of our planet. By knowing the satellites' speed we shall be able to calculate precise measurements of the distances between various points on the globe, thus making the present data more accurate.

"Satellites open new avenues for research in all the earth sciences -- gravimetry and geochemistry, geodesy and geophysics, seismography and hydrology. They will give us important information on the composition of cosmic dust that floats through interstellar space. Science has thus far merely guessed at its nature and properties, but the satellite laboratory will afford the possibility of undertaking a study of this problem from stage to stage. The supposition that cosmic dust is the material out of which planets are formed testifies to the importance of such a laboratory."

Next, I quote a meteorologist: "Air masses that form above ocean areas often determine the weather of land areas. Unfortunately we know so little about these great wastes of water which cover two-thirds of the globe that we know no way to forecast devastating typhoons and tornadoes. Immeasurably broader possibilities for study of the upper reaches of the atmosphere and of its lower regions where weather is made are opened by the creation of the man-made satellite.

"It will be possible to obtain detailed information about the movement and distribution of clouds throughout the globe and, consequently, of the air currents over most of its surface. It is of great value in advancing studies of the general circulation of the terrestrial atmosphere and creating physically substantiated methods for long-range weather forecasts.

"To investigate the complex movements and changes in the atmosphere we must know the earth's albedo, the quantity of energy the earth reflects into space. Satellite observations will supply us with this vitally necessary information. They will also fill in the very scanty data we now have on the density of air at high altitudes, the interaction of the atmospheric layers, and supply other such information with which we can accurately determine the laws of weather formation.

"In addition to having satellites circle the earth at altitudes of several hundred miles, it is desirable to set them spinning at lower altitudes. While these laboratories probably will not function long, they nevertheless can furnish data on the atmosphere around the earth that cannot be obtained from any other source."

My third quotation is from a physicist: "Investigations of diurnal variations, magnetic storms and the phenomena connected with them led scientists to assume that the external magnetic field may be due to systems of electric currents existing beyond the earth. The most likely place where such currents can originate is the ionosphere -- those layers of atmosphere which contain a large number of electrically charged particles. The existence of sources of a magnetic field in the ionosphere has been confirmed by direct magnetic measurements made with rockets. It is also assumed that currents may exist beyond the ionosphere. The source of extra-ionospheric currents may be the charged particles, corpuscles, emitted by the sun, captured by the earth's magnetic field and revolving around the earth in the plane of its magnetic equator.

"Measurements made on satellites will help to verify whether the streams of solar particles are neutral or consist of electrically-charged particles of any given sign. Satellites will also help to verify the existence of extra-ionospheric currents, to obtain data on the ionospheric system of currents, and extend our knowledge of the main part of the magnetic field created by the sources within the earth".

"In studying celestial bodies, we astronomers have always been enormously handicapped because our observatories and scientific stations are at the bottom of the air ocean which envelops the earth, an ocean hundreds of miles deep. We have dreamed of observatories outside the atmosphere and the satellites have brought our dreams closer to reality.

"Now we can confidently predict the construction of satellite observatories within a few years which will circle the earth at an altitude of several thousands of miles and transmit scientific data from interplanetary space. One of the next steps is a rocket capable of penetrating beyond the sphere of terrestrial gravitation, of reaching the vicinity of the moon and circumnavigating it. Such a rocket would give us a wealth of information on the nature of lunar terrain and the structure of the dark side of the moon that is not visible from the earth."

And, finally, this quotation from an astrophysicist: "Cosmic rays travel for countless light years to reach the earth. The energy of particles of cosmic radiation can be expressed only in billions and tens of billions of electron volts. The energy of some particles is even millions of times greater. Research on the how and the where of the original processes which result in creating cosmic rays should be conducted beyond the earth's atmosphere. Otherwise secondary cosmic radiation produced in the atmosphere can be mistaken for primary radiation.

"The satellite laboratory will open new opportunities for study by elminating the distortions produced by the earth's atmosphere. It will be possible to classify the cosmic rays in greater detail according to their mass and energy. This in turn will enable us to find out the mechanism of their origin in the far depths of the cosmos and in our solar system as well.

"It is not unlikely that experiments conducted with the satellite as a vehicle for our instruments will lead to the discovery of new, unknown types of cosmic rays. Various data received from the cosmic ray laboratory above the atmosphere can provide us with an incomparably greater knowledge of the universe than we now have."

These comments about the benefits to civilian science that will result from good use of space vehicles sent on data-gathering missions were made by members of the Academy of Sciences. I should be more specific: by members of the Academy of Sciences of the Union of Soviet Socialist Republics. The Russians are stressing the peaceful uses of space technology as positively and as widely as they can among the nations of the world. My quotations were from a recent issue of the handsome, Life-size magazine -- USSR -- published in well-written English and circulated throughout the United States.

The Russians aren't talking about military missions they propose to assign to their Sputniks. This fact serves to emphasize what we already know -- that in addition to being a new tool of great value to science and to the military, the space vehicle is a device that can be used to great advantage in the vitally important use of psychology and propaganda on a global scale.

Now I should like to return to consideration of the responsibilities of NASA for development, testing, launching, and operation of aeronautical and space vehicles. Over the years, NACA has concentrated for the most part on flight problems in the fields of aerodynamics, propulsion, and structures and structural materials. These are the areas where the NACA has the technical competence and the research tools. Flight into space requires that great effort be devoted also to such problems as electronics, guidance, and physiology or human factors.

It would, of course, be possible for NASA to establish new research centers for study of problems in these last-named areas. Such a procedure would be very costly. Trained people to accomplish the work would have to be recruited; almost certainly they would have to come from scientific and engineering organizations already engaged in work of importance to the national interest. Even more critical would be the passage of months and years before the new laboratories could begin producing information vital to the space programs.

A far wiser course, I believe, will be for NASA to make effective use -- on a contract basis -- of teams of experts and laboratory facilities already in being. Here in Southern California, there are such facilities. As a single example, I would name the Jet Propulsion Laboratory of the California Institute of Technology.

NASA will have to develop new space vehicles. Enormously powerful rocket motors will be required for these space craft; they may be even larger than those required for presently contemplated military missile or space missions. It would be possible for NASA to build the organization and the facilities for such space vehicle and motor design and construction. But again, such action would be very costly and much additional time would be required. It is preferable that design and construction of

- 13 -

these space vehicles and motors be performed, on contract basis, at existing facilities. In such cases, sponsorship might be either by NASA independently or jointly with the Department of Defense.

I am sure that our aircraft industry, so much of which is located in Southern California, is more than casually interested in who may be asked to build the space craft and rocket motors for the civilian program of space exploration and exploitation. One obvious answer is that the organizations best qualified will get the jobs. I would make further observation that when changing military requirements called for production of ballistic and other missiles to supplement the capabilities of the bomber, the aircraft industry demonstrated that its design and production teams were singularly qualified to develop and build missiles.

In recent weeks, to go still further, I have become familiar with many of the satellite and space craft projects proposed by American industry. I haven't counted them. Some say the number is 60. With some poetic license I have put it nearer 200. At any rate, and this is pertinent here, most of these projects are suggested by members of the aircraft industry. So long as the technical and production competence of the industry can keep up with the exploding needs of the space program, the same reasons that discourage construction of new laboratories and scientific teams to perform work that can be done by in-being research organizations would apply to space craft development and construction.

The space programs we will be proposing soon for NASA accomplishment are three-fold in scope. First, there must be adequate research effort on space technology problems. Then there must be development and use of unmanned vehicles capable of carrying the desired scientific data-gathering apparatus. Finally, there must be development and orderly use of man-carrying vehicles in the exploration of our solar system. The three parts of our program must be skillfully integrated and coordinated. Just as rapidly as research can provide the necessary information, we should use it in developing -- and using -- both automated and manned vehicles with greater performance and sophistication.

I should like to emphasize the essentiality of our planning a space program that will be adequate to our needs as a nation. The size of the program and the vigor with which it is carried out must be firmly established and ratified by the Administration, the Congress, and finally, the American people. In making these decisions, we must keep in mind that today Soviet Russia is working harder than we to achieve pre-eminence in the conquest of space.

We must understand that the kind and magnitude of space program that our national interest requires will cost hundreds of millions of dollars each year for many years to come. I know that some knowledgable people fear that although we might be willing to spend a couple of billions for space technology in 1958, because we still remember the humiliation caused by the appearance of the first Sputnik last October, next year we will be so preoccupied by color television, or new style cars, or the beginning of another national election campaign that we'll be unwilling to pay another year's installment on our space conquest bill. For that to happen -- well, I'd just as soon we didn't start.

Fortunately, for the sake of our children's future if not for the protection of our own skins, I don't think we're that grasshopper-minded. This past week I was privileged to appear before the Select Committee on Astronautics and Space Exploration of the House of Representatives. Repeatedly the members of that Committee reflected the wish that I am sure is that of the entire nation, that we determine what is necessary to do to reach our goals in space and then get on with the job.

As a nation, we have the scientific and technical competence. We have the resources to pay the bill. We can and we must succeed in finding our destiny in space.

- END -

The International Geophysical Year

SCIENTISTS OF FORTY-SIX NATIONS STUDY THE LAND, SEA, AND AIR AROUND US

By

Hugh L. Dryden
Director, National Advisory Committee for Aeronautics
Home Secretary, National Academy of Sciences
Trustee, National Geographic Society

We live on the surface of a large roughened ball of rock whirling through space around the kindly sun which furnishes us heat and light. Our every activity is carried out at the bottom of an ocean of air which supplies the oxygen we need to slowly burn the food we eat to give body heat and muscular energy. The scientific study of the motions, heat, light, and electrical properties of our earth, its continents, oceans, and surrounding atmosphere is the science of geophysics.

The scientist in a laboratory may study the laws of Nature under controlled conditions. The earth is too big to bring into a laboratory, and man as yet has little control over storms and earthquakes. The earth scientist can only observe the experiments which Nature makes, and he himself can see only what happens at one place at any one time.

From July, 1957, through December, 1958, some 5000 earth scientists from 46 countries will make a cooperative study of the nature of our earth and its atmosphere. In this International Geophysical Year, or IGY, the scientists will study the atmosphere and oceans from the equator to the poles and from ocean deeps to altitudes of hundreds of miles above the surface. They will measure the puzzling "electric rain" of the cosmic rays that bombard our atmosphere from space and the magnetic storms that hinder radio and telegraph communication.

In this great "symphony of science" the scientists will work as a well-conducted orchestra in harmony. Frequent observations will be made by all participants in each month of IGY on three or four days, called Regular World Days, picked for their coincidence with special phases of the moon. Every quarter during a ten-day World Meteorological Interval, the weather men will redouble their efforts. Whenever the sun shows unusual activity, or the northern aurora lights tower high, or magnetic storms occur, special alerts will be given so that observations may be made over all the earth at the same time.

The International Geophysical Year is the third in a series of International Years, the first being the First International Polar Year of 1882-83. That year contributed much to our knowledge of the "northern lights", the magnificent aurora borealis, that throws across the sky not only an impressive spectacle but also an electrical mirror that interferes with radio reception. From bases set up in the Arctic, new information about Arctic weather and the earth's magnetism were systematically obtained.

The Second International Polar Year, half a century later in 1932-33, brought new knowledge of radio communication and the development of methods of bouncing pulses of radio waves from the ionospher that atmospheric layer from 50 to more than 200 miles above the earth in which ultraviolet light from the sun creates a large number of electrically charged molecules. These techniques were later applied in the development of radar.

After a lapse of only 25 years, interest in the earth sciences had been so great that learned societies around the world, working through their International Council of Scientific Unions, set in motion plans for the 1957-58 International Geophysical Year. Each country plans and carries out its own program under guidance of an international committee. An American, Dr. Lloyd V. Berkner, is president of ICSU and vice-chairman of its special committee on IGY. The National Academy of Sciences has the responsibility for realizing the United States program, using Federal funds obtained through the National Science Foundation. A U. S. National Committee has been established by the Academy with Dr. Joseph Kaplan as its chairman. The Department of Defense, with men and materials, ships, trucks, and planes from each of its three services, is supporting the scientific teams, especially in remote and relatively inaccessible regions.

President Eisenhower has heralded the IGY as "a striking example of the opportunities which exist for cooperative action among the peoples of the world". The U.S.S.R. and at least four other Iron Curtain countries will take part.

The IGY will focus a major effort on the polar regions, especially Antarctica, with its 16,000 miles of little-known coastline. Eleven nations -- Argentina, Australia, Chile, France, Great Britain, Japan, New Zealand, Norway, Union of South Africa, the U.S.S.R., and the United States -- have plans for some 37 stations on Antarctica or its offshore islands. Several nations expect to send expeditions across the cold interior, making scientific observations on the way.

The United States plans six Antarctic observatories, the most remote being at or near the South Pole itself. Already Operation "Deepfreeze I" has accomplished much of the preparatory work. In October, 1956, Operation Deepfreeze II will begin, with reinforcement of the small parties who remained during the winter and the delivery of building materials, food, instruments, and other supplies. Some seventy IGY scientists will proceed to their stations, for the beginning of IGY in July, 1957, is in the middle of the Antarctic winter.

The stations in Antarctica will make daily weather observations both at the surface and to 100,000 feet by means of balloons. The balloons carry radio transmitters to send back reports on temperature, pressure, moisture and wind. Standard magnetic observatories to measure field strength, dip and inclination, will be established at four of the American bases. Gravity measurements will be made on over-snow journeys and airplane flights. Balloon and rocket flights will yield information on cosmic rays which spray the earth constantly, with occasional power bursts far greater than those generated by the biggest man-made atomic accelerators. Holes will be drilled through the Ross Shelf ice and through inland ice to a depth of 1000 feet or more to obtain ice cores and to measure the temperature at various depths for study of the earth's climatic history.

The IGY will emphasize upper-air exploration in an effort to increase our knowledge of the top half of our atmosphere. Much of our surface weather and the efficiency of radio communication are affected by variable conditions in this atmospheric ocean.

A year-long "rocket shoot" will pull new plums of knowledge out of the heavens at heights from 60 to 200 miles above the earth. The United States alone plans to launch hundreds of rockets. Several dozen will be 1250 pound, 20-foot Aerobee-Hi rockets, most of them launched at Fort Churchill, Manitoba, on the west coast of Hudson Bay. Others will blast off from New Mexico.

The United States also intends to launch two-stage rockets -- a combination of the Nike booster and the Deacon rocket -- and several hundred smaller rockets. Some will rise from land sites at Thule,

Greenland, and in central Alaska and some from off the coasts of southern California and Virginia. Others will be launched from ships at sea in numerous locations. Rocket-borne cameras and electronic instruments will provide "eye-witness" reports of conditions on the threshold of space.

On July 29, 1955 President Eisenhower announced that the United States planned, as part of its participation in IGY, to launch into space during 1957 or 1958 history's first artificial earth-circling satellite. The first satellite will weigh approximately 20 pounds and will probably be spherical in shape and between 20 and 30 inches in diameter. It will be launched from the Air Force Missile Test Center at Cape Canaveral, Florida.

A three-stage rocket will be used to place the satellite in an elliptical orbit about the earth, 200 miles from the earth's surface at the nearest point. The first-stage rocket, providing a thrust of 27,000 pounds, will bring the vehicle to a speed between 3000 and 4000 miles per hour. The first stage will then be left behind as the second stage rocket increases the speed to about 11,000 miles per hour at an altitude of about 130 miles. The vehicle then coasts upward until its path becomes approximately horizontal. At this point the third stage rocket is lit and boosts it to the orbital speed of about 18,000 miles per hour.

The satellite then circles the globe every 90 minutes. It is expected to remain in the orbit for a period from several weeks to several months depending on the resistance encountered in the rarefied atmosphere which is not accurately known. Ultimately friction will cause the satellite to spiral inward ~~inward~~ and heat up until it burns like a shooting star.

The earth's atmosphere acts like a screen which prevents us from detecting what happens in the upper atmosphere and in nearby outer space. Dr. Kaplan has called the satellite a "long-playing rocket" because it makes possible the type of observations possible only for minutes or seconds from high altitude rockets for periods of weeks or months. These include the determination of outer atmosphere densities by observation of the air drag effect on the satellite orbit, long-term observations of ultraviolet radiation from the sun, fluctuations in intensity of cosmic rays striking the atmosphere from space, and density of hydrogen atoms and ions in interplanetary space.

The governments and institutions of the several nations that pay the total bill of about 250 million dollars for the IGY program expect and will receive very practical dividends in return. They will enjoy improved weather forecasts and radio communication. They will benefit from greater knowledge of the upper air and nearby space in which airplanes, satellites, and eventually space ships will travel. Moreover, there is the possibility of far greater unsuspected discoveries of who-can-guess-what value to man.

8

The International Geophysical Year will make a significant contribution to man's increasing search for clearer understanding of his surroundings. It will see the first faltering steps toward man's exploration of outer space. It will stir the imagination of countless boys and girls to the wonders and opportunities on the road ahead toward the far horizons of space.
(See "The International Geophysical Year", by Hugh L. Dryden, National Geographic Magazine, February, 1956.)

April 16, 1956

JEROME C. HUNSAKER, Sc. D., CHAIRMAN
ALEXANDER WETMORE, Ph. D., VICE CHAIRMAN

DETLEV W. BRONK, Ph. D.
VICE ADM. JOHN H. CASSADY, U. S. N.
EDWARD U. CONDON, Ph. D.
HON. THOMAS W. S. DAVIS
JAMES H. DOOLITTLE, Sc. D.
RONALD M. HAZEN, B. S.
WILLIAM LITTLEWOOD, M. E.
REAR ADM. THEODORE C. LONNQUEST, U. S. N.

HON. DONALD W. NYROP
MAJ. GEN. DONALD L. PUTT, U. S. A. F.
ARTHUR E. RAYMOND, Sc. D.
FRANCIS W. REICHELDERFER, Sc. D.
MAJ. GEN. GORDON P. SAVILLE, U. S. A. F.
WILLIAM WEBSTER, M. S.
THEODORE P. WRIGHT, Sc. D.

**NATIONAL ADVISORY COMMITTEE
FOR AERONAUTICS**
1724 F STREET, NORTHWEST
WASHINGTON 25, D. C.

TELEPHONE: LIBERTY 5-6700

LANGLEY AERONAUTICAL LABORATORY
LANGLEY FIELD, VA.

AMES AERONAUTICAL LABORATORY
MOFFETT FIELD, CALIF.

LEWIS FLIGHT PROPULSION LABORATORY
CLEVELAND AIRPORT, CLEVELAND 11, OHIO

TRENDS IN NACA RESEARCH AND DEVELOPMENT

By

Hugh L. Dryden, Director
National Advisory Committee for Aeronautics

Presented at SAE National Aeronautics Meeting
Biltmore Hotel, Los Angeles, California
October 5, 1951

For the third time in its history, the trend of NACA research and development is heavily toward the support of the military aeronautical program, which is the chief hope for the preservation of the peace of the world. Over the years since the creation of the Committee as an independent agency of the government to "supervise and direct the scientific study of the problems of flight with a view to their practical solution", there has evolved an intimate relationship between the aircraft industry, the military agencies, and NACA, such that the contributions of each group are thoroughly interwoven with those of the others in the final product. All work together to attain superiority in performance and military effectiveness of our air weapons.

NACA has been primarily responsible for the conduct of an adequate research program to lay the groundwork for continuing progress by the designer and builder. This assignment of primary responsibility has not meant that no one else should perform research nor that NACA was restricted from completing work on some problem by testing its research findings by practical application.

Numerous university groups engage in fundamental research in the aeronautical sciences. The NACA led in sponsoring aeronautical research by educational groups, and today supports almost a million dollars worth of such work each year. Support of research performed by universities is also forthcoming from the military services, and the military services themselves conduct a great deal of research, especially in such fields as electronics, armament, aeromedicine, geophysics, and others not within the scope of NACA's responsibility. The aircraft industry, the airplane and engine manufacturers also conduct research. There is an exchange of programs, results, and views and a resulting correlation and coordination of research effort in the NACA executive committee and its twenty-seven technical subcommittees and in the committees of the Research and Development Board of the Department of Defense.

Let us examine a little more closely how the work of the NACA ties in directly with the planning and procurement of the military services in the field of aircraft and missiles. The start of such planning and procurement is, I suppose, a blueprint of what will have to be done to make good the military commitments of the United States. These commitments include the defense of the continental United States and our other territories, the support we have promised to the defense of those European nations who wish to live in a free world, and a successful completion of the action in Korea.

Next comes the writing of the specifications for the airplanes and missiles and power plants which will be needed, as well as the many other weapons and items of equipment for which NACA has no responsibility.

In the establishment of requirements for aircraft and missiles, and the specifications to meet them, NACA counsels as to what kind of performance the manufacturers should be able to design and build into the models ordered. Today they can make fighter airplanes that flirt with the speed of sound, using the 7,000-pound-thrust engines which are manufactured today. Tomorrow, on the basis of new aeronautical knowledge built up since today's airplanes were conceived, they can design and manufacture supersonic airplanes with qualities which the military need in tactically useful airplanes. Sometimes, perhaps, the industry must think that the counsel we give the military services is altogether too optimistic, but we are ready to roll up our sleeves to help make good on the projects embodying the frontiers of knowledge, and the industry has a way of translating the possibilities into actualities.

Then comes the design competition. Here NACA's contribution is to supply the results of basic and applied research which bear on the problems which the designer must solve. The design of aircraft is an art, the art of securing the best compromise between the desired and the possible. Unfortunately, the aircraft which is designed for maximum speed has reduced range and reduced maneuverability and similarly conflicts arise in many other aspects of the design problem. Ingenuity and inventive application are necessary ingredients of a successful prototype. Yet the designer must base his solutions on sound technical knowledge, and a great deal of this knowledge can be supplied by NACA. If we are on the job, we will foresee the problems of the future and work toward their solution to be ready when the designer needs the information. We review the state of knowledge for him in technical conferences and we advise on the special problems of his design.

The design proposals are evaluated by the military services and one or more contracts awarded for prototypes. In practically every important project the military services at some stage request the use of NACA equipment and skills on specific problems. Models are constructed as the engineering work progresses for measurements in high-speed wind tunnels at large Reynolds numbers, and for rocket-propelled model tests. Power plants under development are installed and operated in the altitude tanks under conditions encountered in flight at high altitude. Engineers of the company whose models are under test are on hand, and, as the information is secured, modifications are considered. In every case it is the company engineer who decides what, if any, changes will be made. We are as helpful as possible, but NACA is not in the business of designing or constructing airplanes. There is more than enough research to be done.

Then the prototype flies. If you think the research and development job is then finished, let me tell you the story in terms of one of the best airplanes to be built during the last war. Up to and through the prototype stage, the manufacturer invested something like a million and a half engineering man-hours in this airplane. During this same period, NACA spent almost a hundred thousand engineering man-hours on the airplane. During the period this airplane was in production - and a good many of this particular model were built - the manufacturer spent almost five million engineering man-hours to secure improvements. During the same period NACA spent approximately a half-million man-hours to the same end.

In this life cycle of an airplane, so unfamiliar to the lay public not associated with it, there are encountered the three principal categories of NACA research. The first is the truly basic research, the exploration of new fields, and the search for more complete understanding of older fields. This is the work which can lead to radically new developments and which will pay off in the design of future aircraft and power plants. Our present aircraft embody the results of basic research carried out years ago which now seems so familiar to the designer that he forgets it was ever new.

The second category is applied research directed at the foreseen problems of the aircraft now being designed. The problems to be worked on are crystallized from the thinking of designers, users, and research workers. This is the research which can be swiftly translated into practice, embodied in actual aircraft at an early date, granted only that sufficient manpower and funds are provided. This is the work which makes possible an increase in thrust of the next engine, and improved stability and controllability of the next airplane.

The third category is specific research on the problems of the prototypes now building or flying. The problems encountered in a production airplane automatically assume top priority; those of a prototype produce equal pressures. This work is essentially a part of the development of the specific airplane or missile.

The three categories differ principally in the time scale and, as is natural in a period of tension and large production of aircraft, the trend of NACA research is toward a shorter term on the average. This trend has some elements of danger, and I wish to discuss briefly current consideration of NACA research policy and its implementation. It will be recalled that ten years ago just prior to World War II, the pressure on NACA to concentrate on applying available scientific knowledge to the immediate improvement of airplanes scheduled for war production soon became so great that the basic research programs were cut and cut until they represented hardly 10 percent of our total work. The result was that we came out of that war with a serious deficiency of research information, especially in supersonic aerodynamics and jet propulsion.

The trend to short-term specific investigations must not occur again to the same degree as during World War II. To do so will undermine the research foundation upon which our future development program must be built. In the current situation of a probable extended period of international tension and the dependence of the free world on the leadership of the United States we must continue the program of fundamental scientific research initiated after the close of World War II and at the same time provide for the speedy refinement of production airplane designs, the correction of troubles, and the essential day-to-day improvement of current types. This is the stated policy of NACA reflected in its budget submissions and operating practices. Its full implementation is contingent on increased financial support and the continued sympathetic consideration of the military agencies in the calling up of reservists and of the draft boards in the deferment of specialized personnel.

The experience of thirty-six years has taught that a moderate effort on specific investigations of current airplanes and missiles insures a more realistic and effective conduct of the basic and applied research, promotes mutual understanding between research scientists and designers, and secures early application of research results. It is greatly in the national interest that the knowledge and skills of NACA scientists be brought to bear on the critical problems of current prototype and production airplanes and missiles.

It is too much to expect that any citizen, even an NACA research scientist, administrator, or Committee member will refuse to help make our present airplanes as good as they can be made. What is required is a balanced effort within a total effort commensurate with the need The total effort, in manpower and money, needed for the research and development to insure the qualitative superiority of our air weapons is small relative to the total effort being expended to build up our air power.

At least by comparison, NACA is in a better position today to undertake this double-barreled task than on the eve of World War II. Then we had one laboratory, and something less than 600 research scientists and supporting personnel. Today we have three laboratories, and a little more than 7,000 research scientists and supporting personnel. With the research equipment we now have, or are in the process of acquiring, we should have most of the essential tools. Inevitably we shall have to increase the number of our people, perhaps by 50 percent, but nothing like the way we had to expand a decade ago. In the light of the tremendous technical changes brought about by jet propulsion and consequent supersonic speeds, the innumerable new problems added to the old ones, and the three-fold expansion of the military research and development program, such a modest expansion of NACA effort may appear too small. The expansion is in fact limited by the saturation of use of critical facilities and shortages of technical manpower rather than by the needs of the expanded military program.

The trends in research policy which have just been described are reflections of the trend of technical developments in the aeronautical sciences and their applications to airplanes and missiles now being designed. These technical trends can be discussed in an unclassified paper only in very general terms, and space limits the discussion to a few examples.

The first obvious trend is that toward aircraft of greatly increased performance. It seems probable that airplane speeds may be increased as much in the next five years as in the whole history of human flight up to World War II. Experimental flights with piloted aircraft at transonic and supersonic speeds have been made with increased frequency during the past year. It has been clearly demonstrated that aircraft operations will ultimately be conducted throughout the entire transonic range. Information is becoming available to permit the development of airplanes capable of further penetration of the transonic and low supersonic speed ranges with fewer operational limitations. The limited successes already realized have brought to light many detailed problems which can be solved by continued research. These relate to all phases of transonic and supersonic stability, control, maneuverability, and performance, and the landing and take-off behavior of the new and unconventional high-speed configurations. An exceptionally important development is the transonic ventilated wind-tunnel throat invented by Stack and his associates, which makes possible the study of transonic problems in wind tunnels, hitherto impossible because of the choking of the conventional wind tunnel as the speed approaches the speed of sound. All high-speed wind tunnels in this country will be converted to transonic operation as rapidly as the necessary funds are supplied. Tremendous improvements in the aerodynamic characteristics of aircraft configurations at transonic and supersonic speeds have already been made, including large drag reductions and imporved stability and control. A striking feature of the results is the sensitivity to details of design which forecasts a necessity for much additional specific testing.

Technical development is moving in a direction to throw heavier responsibility on the structures design group. Structural problems may become a limiting feature in the future and NACA is taking steps to secure the necessary tools and to place increased effort in this area. The requirements of long-range, high-speed, high-altitude operations often result in a relatively flexible airplane structure. This gives rise to important mutural interactions between aerodynamic loads and structural deflection, as well as to important transient dynamic loads in gusty air and on landing. Furthermore, the flexible structure may vibrate unduly or exhibit the catastrophic phenomenon of flutter. These phenomena may be studied by investigations of dynamically similar models as well as by more fundamental studies of the component aerodynamic and structural behavior under dynamic conditions. A second structural problem which will in time become the major problem limiting further gains in airplane performance is that of the distortion of the structure and changes in physical properties of materials arising from the heating of the surface of high-speed aircraft and missiles.

The dependence of missiles on automatic stabilization and control and guidance equipment has led to more intensive study of the matching of the aerodynamic characteristics to the characteristics of the automatic equipment. Similar problems are now arising in piloted aircraft, where the high performance places demands on the pilot beyond his physical capacities. His vision is extended by radar, his muscles by power boost in the control system, and his slow reaction time is compensated by automatic equipment. Furthermore, automatic equipment can be used to improve the flying qualities of aircraft, even when there is no question of supplementing the physical abilities of the pilot. This trend in technical development yields a host of new problems as well as the opportunity for increasing the utility of high-performance aircraft.

Recent improvements in gas-turbine-engine performance through adoption of afterburners on turbojet engines for thrust augmentation have complicated the problem of engine control. The technical characteristics of jet engines require operation near the safe limits of speed and temperature. Application of turbine-propeller engines likewise presents a control problem which places an intolerable burden on the operator unless quick-acting, accurate, stable, and safe control systems are fitted to the engines. The solution of these problems requires equipment for operating the complete system under altitude conditions and the use of analogue computers for rapid study of the effects of design changes.

In order to obtain high performance, the hot parts of jet engines are made of high-termperature alloys which contain alloying metals either not found in the United States or in limited supply. A major trend in engine development is the reduction of strategic material content to permit large-scale production. An important part of NACA research is devoted to this problem, ranging from basic research on why materials behave as they do to substitute materials and to turbine blade cooling. Turbine blade cooling offers promise either of removing practically all of the strategic materials from the blades while retaining present performance or of substantially increasing output for applications for which the strategic materials can be allocated in sufficient quantity.

As another illustration of the trend in technical development, mention may be made of the increased attention being given to the research underlying the development of helicopters of improved performance which has resulted from the great utility of this type of aircraft demonstrated in recent military operations. Attention is being given to high-speed rotors, jet rotors, stability and control of multi-rotor helicopters, flying qualities, and vibration characteristics.

The pattern of technical development has changed very decidedly since the days of World War II. Progress in performance then proceeded at what now seems to be a relatively slow and orderly pace. A reasonable goal was a speed advance of 100 miles per hour or less or a modest increase in rate of climb or altitude. The engineering advances required were modest, and much effort was devoted to the study of changes which increased the maximum speed 20 or 30 miles per hour. The problems of compressibility effects were still new and the sonic barrier seemed very real. Much effort produced a little closer approach to the critical Mach number.

Today we are contemplating, and with some assurance of success, striving toward very large gains in performance. The chance of success is greatly dependent on extensive detailed knowledge; small changes of contour may make large changes in performance. The design compromises are much more difficult than before. As a result we have found that the step-up in military research and development leads first to demands for expedited applied research in many critical areas and at a much later stage to requests for tests of specific configurations. The problems are so many, and the cost of failure to advance so great, that accelerated effort in the critical problem areas is a priceless insurance.

These then are some of the trends of NACA research and development to meet NACA's responsibility in the current situation. We of NACA pool our skills with those of our industry and military colleagues to increase greatly the military strength of the United States and its allies with the hope of maintaining peace by deterring aggression. If, nevertheless, war should come, the joining of a great research and development potential with demonstrated production abilities will bring us victory. To these efforts of free men to maintain their freedom, we of NACA will give our best.

* * * * * * * * *

October 5, 1951

THE DAWN OF THE SUPERSONIC AGE

Hugh L. Dryden
Director of Aeronautical Research
National Advisory Committee for Aeronautics

(Lecture delivered at the University of California, Berkeley, May 24, 1948 and Los Angeles, May 25, 1948)

It is a great honor and pleasure to be invited to give one of the public lectures in your engineering lecture series. This lecture will not be a technical paper in the usual sense and has none of the usual appurtenances of such papers. It is in part an attempt to interpret the aims, goals, and effects in human affairs of one field of development in aeronautical engineering; in part an attempt to give you a nodding acquaintance with some of the current technical problems in that field.

Last week while I was standing with a group of aeronautical engineers on the lawn of the Inn at Williamsburg, Virginia, there was heard that new and never-to-be-forgotten sound, the high pitched swish of a jet-propelled aircraft somewhere in the sky. Everyone began to use their natural sound locators, turning the head back and forth to obtain equal intensity of sound in the two ears and looking straight ahead to locate the source, but no airplane was to be seen. Then a wiser and more experienced operator called out "You have to look ahead of the sound" and sure enough by looking a considerable distance ahead of the apparent origin of the sound, the airplane was readily located. The jet airplane travels at such a large fraction of the speed of sound that in the time required for the sound to travel the distance from the airplane to the observer, the airplane has moved a comparable distance along its path.

In London during the last war the inhabitants were harassed by two types of distinctive missiles. The buzz-bomb traveling much slower than the speed of sound telegraphed its coming long in advance, holding its victims in terrifying suspense. The V-2 rocket traveling several times faster than sound was more merciful. No warning sound was propagated and the victims never knew what happened. The survivors saw the explosion and only afterward heard the noise arising at successive points along the path in reverse order, much like a phonograph record played backwards.

These human experiences have brought into our daily speech a familiarity with the use of the speed of sound as a measure of comparison for the speeds of aircraft and missiles and with the new words coined by scientists, sonic speed for a speed equal to that of sound; subsonic speed for speeds less than that of sound; supersonic speed for speeds greater than that of sound; transonic speed for speeds just below and above the speed of sound especially for objects which pass <u>through</u> the speed of sound in their travel; and Mach number, the ratio of the speed of the aircraft or missile to the speed of sound.

The scientist uses the sonic speed as his measure not because of the difference in travel of sound to an observer, previously described, but because he finds by experiment that the laws of air flow are greatly different for subsonic and supersonic speeds. George W. Gray, in his book on Frontiers of

Flight, which is a history of the wartime work of the National Advisory Committee for Aeronautics, recounts the story of an American fighter pilot during the last war who dove his airplane steeply toward the earth in pursuit of a German fighter plane. After shooting down the German plane, he attempted to pull back on the control stick to level out from the dive. But the stick resisted and seemed held in a vice. With all his strength he struggled, but the airplane continued downward at high speed. As he was ready to abandon ship the elevator suddenly took hold and the plane curved out of the dive with high acceleration. This new and baffling experience arose from the fact that the speed of the airplane was reaching a speed at which the air was flowing locally over parts of the wings and tail at speeds faster than sound although the airplane itself was traveling at only three-quarters the speed of sound.

Why did the airplane recover at all? The explanation is that the speed of sound changes as the temperature of the air changes. Near the ground in the warm air at sea level it is about 760 miles per hour. In the upper atmosphere where the temperature is about $-55°$ F. the speed of sound is only 660 miles per hour. Thus as the airplane dived, its speed, decreasing slowly because of the increasing density of the air, became smaller in comparison with the speed of sound and the adverse effects disappeared.

The great task confronting the NACA, university, industrial, and other government research laboratories is the prompt exploration of the laws of airflow in the transonic and supersonic regions. The task of the designers of military aircraft is to apply this knowledge to build aircraft which may fly safely at these speeds. Many existing aircraft can enter the transonic region, at least in dives. For security reasons I do not expect to tell you exactly the limits of speed which have been reached under various conditions. I can state that we are at the dawn of the supersonic age in the sense that many aircraft now flying, travel at such high speeds that the air flows locally past their wings at speeds faster than sound and that it is only a matter of time before sustained horizontal supersonic flight of piloted aircraft will be a commonplace event, as the dawn is superseded by the full sunlight of the oncoming day. I am on record as having predicted last fall that the sunrise of the new age will occur before the end of the calendar year 1946. Some newspaper men say it has already occurred. In the present international climate I predict a cloudy sunrise and there will be some difficulty in determining exactly when the dawn turns to day.

The impact of engineering development in aeronautics on our civilization has from the beginning been very great. Airplanes of ever increasing performance have served our civilization usefully. At first flying was the hazardous occupation of a few men who capitalized on the danger to entertain and to thrill the many by aerial circuses and races. Some more far-seeing pilots began to demonstrate the peacetime utility by pioneering in aerial photography, crop dusting, the carrying of mail, passengers, and freight. These peacetime useful services of aviation have grown to large size and aircraft are indispensable to our economy. It is possible to do things which were impossible before, for example, I could leave Washington Sunday afternoon, speak in Berkeley on Monday evening, Los Angeles Tuesday evening, and be back in Washington on Wednesday evening.

You will recall the introduction of the airplane as a military weapon in World War I and its rapid development to become today the Keystone of our national security. It is the pressing claim of this use of the airplane that has brought the dawn of the supersonic age as we shall later discuss.

These are the direct contributions to the machinery of daily living and fighting. But the indirect contributions to man's intellectual and spiritual life are even more striking. Aeronautical developments have endless ramifications in the daily lives and mental processes of all of us, engineers, educators, business men, John Q. Public, or however else we may wish to classify ourselves or our major interests. Aeronautical engineering has left its impress on other branches of engineering as well as on society as a whole. In these times we cannot afford as engineers to ignore this consequence of our work and in this discussion I do not propose to ignore the human aspects of our technical work.

I may illustrate the way in which a complex technical development can affect the life of the average man by reviewing very briefly an earlier age of aeronautical development, the streamline age. You probably recall the early airplane, usually a wood, wire, and fabric creation with exposed struts, wires, engine, landing gear, and passengers. You probably remember the development of the cantilever monoplane, of the cowling of the aircooled engines, of the retractable landing gear, all greatly reducing the drag and increasing the speed. Perhaps you have seen the flow of smoke or water around objects of various shapes and are familiar with the concept of a streamline body as a body which moves through the air or water leaving behind it the least possible disturbance. You know that your automobile or a train is not really a good streamline body because of the cloud of dust and debris stirred up by its passage. Although the development of streamlined aircraft has been carried to a high point even to the removal of rivet heads on the exterior surface, and the principle has been in part applied to automobiles and trains, surely the more important influence has been on the intellectual and spiritual lives of men. And by that I do not refer particularly to the rather facetious and frivolous application of the adjective "streamline" in advertising to furnaces, washing machines, flat irons, women's stockings, men's shirts, and the female figure, but to the more solid and meaningful concept of that harmony with the physical laws of the universe which enables us to live with a minimum of useless effort and disturbance. The streamlining of office procedures, of the Committees of Congress, of specifications for materials, of college curricula; -- all such concepts grew out of this impact of the aeronautical engineering development of an aircraft which traveled through the air with a minimum of disturbance, with each part functional and operating at peak efficiency. I have heard also in government bureaus of streamlining the buck so that it may more readily be passed from one office to another. But surely more important than all of these is the streamlining of one's life so that we may proceed with a minimum of friction with our neighbors, with our energies applied to the task of reaching our goals swiftly.

In similar fashion I assert that the supersonic age will profoundly affect the lives of all of you, physically, mentally, and spiritually and hence you should become familiar at this early date with this oncoming technical development.

Let us look at some of the technical problems to be solved in the development of supersonic piloted aircraft. In general terms the problems arise from the radical changes in the aerodynamic relationships at speeds faster than sound as compared with those prevailing at speeds slower than sound. A reasonably satisfactory design could now be made to operate at any one value of the speed, subsonic or supersonic, if the transonic region of mixed flow is avoided. However, any practical airplane must be able to take off and land and hence must be able to fly satisfactorily in both the subsonic and supersonic regimes and also during the passage through the transonic region. In fact, it would be desirable to be able to fly steadily in the transonic region as well.

The first problem is that of providing a powerplant of sufficiently high thrust to overcome the drag or resistance to motion at supersonic speeds. Ballisticians many years ago found that the resistance to motion of a projectile increased disproportionately as the speed of sound was approached, the drag increasing much faster than the square of the speed. About 20 years ago experiments in which I had some part showed that the drag coefficient of an airplane wing increased suddenly many fold and the lift coefficient decreased very greatly in the transonic region. These findings have repeatedly been confirmed. The development of jet and rocket propulsion has now given us powerplants of large thrust in a relatively small package. There are three types of jet powerplants available or under development; the turbo-jet, the ram-jet, and the rocket, each producing thrust as the result of squirting a hot jet of air to the rear. Any boy who has blown up a toy balloon and let it escape from his hands has observed jet propulsion and therefore can understand it. As a matter of fact, the conventional airplane propeller operates by producing a jet. In the newer engines heat is used to produce the jet. The rocket carries both fuel and oxygen, i.e., all the elements required for a chemical reaction to produce heat, transform the fuel and oxidant to hot gas, and eject the products of combustion. It therefore can operate anywhere, under water, in the air or outside the earth's atmosphere.

Turbo-jet and ram-jet engines get their oxygen from the atmosphere, as does the conventional reciprocating engine. The turbo-jet uses a mechanical compressor to compress the air and a turbine to drive the compressor. In the ram-jet compression is produced by the rapid motion of the vehicle; hence a ram-jet propelled vehicle must be brought to a high speed by other means, for example, booster rockets.

The new powerplants give a great deal of power per pound of weight and have the desirable characteristic that the power increases with the speed. In his book Gray gives the following figures at a speed of 750 miles per hour for certain powerplants Rocket 53.7 horsepower per pound; ram-jet 6.9 horsepower per pound; turbo-jet 3.5 horsepower per pound. However, at the same speed the rocket burns 8.3 pounds of fuel per horsepower hour; the ram-jet 2.8; the turbo-jet 1.0. The relative merits of the engine types are complicated functions of the speed and altitude of flight. Suffice it to say that these powerplants furnish sufficient power to drive aircraft at supersonic speeds. Much research is required to improve their efficiency, reliability, and limits of operation as regards speed and altitude.

The converse of the problem of producing sufficient thrust is reduction of drag. Here again considerable progress has been made. The introduction of sweptback wings heralds the new-look for high-speed aircraft, although all airplanes having sweepback do not necessarily travel at supersonic speeds. Sweepback is highly advantageous in the transonic region. At supersonic speeds model tests indicate advantages for a triangular planform or short stubby thin wings.

The drag can be greatly reduced by reducing the density of the air by traveling at high altitude, but as is well known, high altitude flight introduces new problems both for the human occupant and the powerplant. As the density is reduced, a greater and greater volume of air must be forced through the engine to supply the necessary oxygen to burn the fuel in the case of the ram-jet and turbo-jet. It becomes more and more difficult to maintain the conditions needed for combustion, to "keep the fire lit" in the parlance of the jet pilot. Research workers are busily engaged on these questions. It is obvious that supersonic flight near the ground will be extremely costly in fuel, and that economy and efficiency is to be obtained by high altitude flight. Hence the interest today in determining the physical properties of the air at very high altitudes by means of sounding rockets, and in reproducing these conditions in the laboratory for studying the problems to be encountered in high-speed flight in the upper atmosphere. Professor Folsom and his associates here at the University of California are doing pioneering work in this field.

Perhaps the most difficult technical problems are those relating to control and stability. At subsonic speeds the lifting force on a wing acts through a point about one-quarter the distance from the leading edge to the trailing edge; at supersonic speeds it acts through a point half the distance from leading to trailing edge. Thus there are sudden changes in the trim of the airplane in the transonic region. There are also changes in the stability, produced partly by the change in the airflow at the tail produced by the loss of lift. A number one research problem is to find configurations which go through the transonic region with minimum changes in trim, control, and stability.

Research has shown that disturbances known as shock waves develop in the flow near the wing at transonic speeds and that these shock waves are often accompanied by flow separation. When this occurs the air flows past the wing with violent fluctuations shaking or buffeting the wing and if the wing wake strikes the tail, the tail structure may be subjected to violent irregularly varying loads sufficient to produce structural damage. A knowledge of buffeting loads and, if possible, the design of wing sections and configurations which avoid flow separation are necessary to develop aircraft to fly safely in the transonic region.

The configurations which seem best for flight at supersonic speeds usually show poor landing characteristics. Much research is needed on methods for improving these characteristics by use of suitable flaps or by methods as yet unknown.

At high speeds the loads on the wings and tail are large and produce deflections, twisting, and bending of the structure. These distortions change the air loads and there is thus a complicated interaction between aerodynamic and structural design. For example, the deflection of the aileron to correct a disturbance in roll may twist the wing enough to counteract the desired effect of the aileron, thus increasing the disturbance. Difficult aeroelastic problems must be solved by the designer.

It is well known that meteors traveling through the air at high supersonic speeds get so hot from friction with the air that their surface melts. At lower supersonic speeds the heating is by no means negligible and is already receiving consideration even at subsonic speeds. In a piloted aircraft the cabin or cockpit must be kept at a reasonable temperature say less than 100° F. Refrigeration is required at speeds as low as 500 miles per hour, partly because of aerodynamic heating, but partly because of radiation from the sun. In a pilotless aircraft or missile the temperature could be permitted to go somewhat higher but ultimately a point is reached at which mechanical and electrical devices will not function or the structural properties of the materials are greatly deteriorated by the high temperature. Whether or not a piloted supersonic airplane can be flown at high supersonic speeds may be determined by the results of research on methods of cooling the cabin and the structure.

These technical problems are being attacked by many new and ingenious tools, the best known being the wind tunnel. The first supersonic experiments with which I am familiar were made in 1890 in a jet about a quarter of an inch in diameter, the flow lasting about three seconds. Now there are supersonic wind tunnels 1 foot by 3 feet in cross section in regular operation and others 6 feet by 6 feet and 6 feet by 8 feet approaching completion. Techniques for measurements on objects dropped from aircraft at high altitudes and on rockets fired from the ground at supersonic speeds have yielded much valuable information. Still another method is to place a model in the local region of supersonic flow on the upper surface of the wing of an airplane traveling at high subsonic speeds, a method devised by Mr. Gilruth of the NACA. The same technique was applied by Lockheed and by the NACA by installing a bump in a subsonic wind tunnel.

So much for the purely technical aspects. Why does anyone wish to travel faster than sound? Dr. von Karman once closed a technical lecture with this question and stated that the reply must be left to the philosopher, but all of us must be, to some extent, philosophers, if amateur ones. There is no question

- 13 -

but that the primary motive of our nation in devoting large sums of money and time to accomplish supersonic flight is the desire for national security. The dominant position of air power as an element in national security has been thoroughly demonstrated. Speed has always been that element of performance of an aircraft which makes it possible to control the air. We have been told by our military leaders that had Hitler grasped the significance of the development of turbo-jet and rocket-propelled aircraft and exploited them, our bomber missions could not have continued as then operated over Germany. All of us observed the inability of England to defend itself against supersonic V-2 missiles, once the missiles were launched. Speed is the major characteristic of the fighter and intercepter and speed is the most important defensive armament of the bomber. There now seems to be no technical obstacle which cannot be overcome by research and the fear that some other nation may produce faster aircraft which could outrun our own aircraft in the sky is the powerful incentive to desire to travel faster than sound.

Finally as to why fly faster than sound, I will not have you discount the value of speed in commercial air transport when accompanied by safety and reliability. It now takes about twelve hours elapsed time to cross the continent, and the trip is very comfortable in modern aircraft. Nevertheless, it would be still more comfortable if it could be done in three or four hours. It is easy to predict that this will surely come; it is harder to predict the timing. Over the years the speed of commercial air transport operation has lagged the airplane speed record by 15 or 20 years. Hence we might estimate that in 1968 the speed of commercial air transports would be about 650 mph, the present speed record. But the jet engine has introduced a discontinuity, the possibility of a sharp rise in the rate of development, and hence this performance may come earlier. There are many optimists who day dream about aeronautical progress without adequate technical support for their predictions and there are also more sober and solidly-based predictions. The conservative predictions have usually been outstripped. As recently as 1940 Archibald Black, an aviation writer, made the following statement: "It has been estimated that if it were possible to build an airplane that could fly at more than 800 miles per hour, the rocket principle might then be promising. This speed, however, is yet too fantastic to be considered even as a future possibility, although it is always dangerous to say of anything in aviation that 'it will never come'." This speed does not now seem so far away. Research today on speeds faster than sound is research on the commercial air transport of the future.

The achievements of aeronautical engineering have had a stimulating effect on other branches of engineering. The supersonic age will influence the training of all engineers as well as contribute to developments in mechanical and electrical engineering. Solution of the manifold problems of supersonic flight requires both an increasing specialization of individual engineers and improved methods of synthesizing the efforts of specialists toward a common goal. There is need for men who have detailed mastery in such diverse fields as organic chemistry (for fuels for turbo-jets, ram-jets, and rockets), metallurgy, ceramics (for heat-resistant materials), dynamics of structures (vibration and flutter problems), electronics (for instruments and control devices), servomechanisms (for autopilots, gunsights, and guelaying), aerodynamics, thermodynamics, and many others. There must be experts in the borderline fields, such as aeroelastic problems, aerothermodynamics, etc. Each of these is a field in which the body of knowledge and experience is steadily growing and each requires the full time energy of anyone for its mastery.

The work of specialists must be integrated to an extent not required in other branches of engineering. Engineers in other fields have successfully met the problems of large enterprises, planning the flow of materials, arranging for matching of characteristics of components, securing dimensional agreement of mating parts. In most of these fields the problems can be broken down readily for solution, with the coordination requiring only small adjustments. In a supersonic aircraft or missile, each special problem reacts on all the others to an extent demanding a new type and higher order of coordination. For example, such an apparently simple thing as the design of a radar antenna cannot be adequately treated without consideration of the effects on the aerodynamic characteristics and hence on the required powerplant. A suitable compromise must be worked out between many conflicting requirements. A group of leaders must be trained who can intelligently make these compromises. They must be men with broad training in many fields with mastery of mathematical and experimental methods of analysis of complex problems, and with a certain boldness of venture.

Aeronautical engineers engaged in work on guided missiles have learned the great stimulus of boldly attempting to design an operating missile. Granting that all the desired basic research has not been completed, the attempt to sink or swim in the venture reveals what the key problems really are and in conjunction with rational mathematical analysis enables the development effort to be concentrated on the real obstacles to progress. Engineers must be taught to use the coordinated experimental and theoretical attack on their problems to utilizing the skills of specialists, and to weigh, balance, and evaluate the data obtained from all. Such is the mode of operation of the engineer in a supersonic age.

The supersonic age will also make its imprint on the average man. As in the case of the atomic bomb, the supersonic age will at first bring fear to his mind because of its portent for war. Engineers are prone to direct attention to the material benefits of their creations to the public, to the power of many slaves which they have supplied to do physical labor, to their contributions to ease and comfort, and they are equally prone to ignoré the common belief that scientific and technical developments appear often to bring misfortune. The truth, of course, is that material things are neither good nor evil; they may be used for either purpose by good or evil men. The same chemical compound brings you the blessing of clean white shirts and the curse of a poisonous gas to be used in war. Another gives you broad, paved streets, mines your coal, or crumbles buildings and cities. The supersonic age likewise is in itself neither a blessing nor a curse. It may be either.

The faster transport of the supersonic age will dissolve barriers of time and space and the world will shrink still more, increasing the pressure for solution of many social, political, and economic problems. When man can outrun the sun and arrive at his destination before he leaves, as measured by the sun, he must obtain a new perspective of international and sectional problems.

The supersonic age will bring a lifting of intellectual horizons as having conquered the space and time limitations of this world, he seeks new worlds to conquer. He will begin to think more seriously about the exploration of the high upper atmosphere and to wonder whether the exploration of outer space is not more than a figment of the human imagination.

But man must not be too impatient. He has climbed far. The realization of his dreams requires the time and effort of many, perhaps even of generations. And you and I can only regret that we cannot linger to see of what stuff these dreams are made.

3/12/50

THE IMPORTANCE OF RELIGION IN AMERICAN LIFE

To be an American citizen, a participant in molding the affairs of a nation devoted to the cause of liberty and freedom is a coveted privilege and a just cause for pride. However, the privilege carries with it a heavy responsibility not only for defending and maintaining those essentially Christian principles by word of mouth but also for exemplifying them within our own lives. We say that we are a Christian nation, a religious people, but any reasonably honest observer will find much to cast doubt on the accuracy of this claim. Yet a man or woman without religious faith is an incomplete man or woman, crippled and deformed, stunted, unworthy of a high destiny. Intended to walk the earth as great souls with great ideas, great dreams, and great accomplishments, many dwarf their world and themselves.

One night in New York on the subway I asked a man, "What is the nearest station to 181st Street? I am not too familiar with the stations up that way." He said, "I don't know." "You don't know. Do you ride this line regularly?" "I ride it every night." "Don't you know the nearest station to 181st Street?" "No," he said, "I never go above 168th Street." His daily world, he explained, was from 168th Street to 34th Street. If such a person is not careful he may get the 34th Street to 168th Street mind after awhile. You can live in the greatest city in the world and become awfully little by allowing your horizons to shrink and your visions of the great world to shrivel.

> "The world stands out on either side
> No wider than the heart is wide;
> Above the world is stretched the sky,
> No higher than the soul is high.
> The heart can push the sea and land
> Farther away on either hand;
> The soul can split the sky in two,
> And let the face of God shine through.
> But East and West will pinch the heart
> That cannot keep them pushed apart,
> And the soul that's flat
> The sky will cave in on by-and-by".
>   Renascence, by Edna St. Vincent Millay

A superficial examination of our society shows a world in which men have achieved longer life and better health, more gadgets and luxuries, freedom from toil and greater leisure. For millions many of these achievements are still only a hope, better living a long way off. The machine and factory are taskmasters. Men flock to her together in great cities, creating a mass society, possessed of a crowd mind.

The monotony of living and working by the clock and of having one's activities geared to mass production, has unbalanced men's emotions, frayed their nerves, and made them the victims of fads, fashions, and demagogues. Class and race hatreds have been aggravated. Things are in abundance but not available to all.

We live in an amazing age of science and technology with a jungle legacy of selfishness, lust, and hate, dark passions of human nature, little changed from the time of Adam. We have harnessed the powers of the physical world around us, steam, electricity, chemical reaction and some nuclear reactions, we have erected towering cities, conquered barriers of space and time by automobile, railroad, airplane, telegraph, and radio. Through science each of us may have the equivalent of 30 slaves sweating for him without the suffering and shame of human slavery. Poverty can be replaced with wealth without robbing the poor or taxing the rich. Yet an ever-increasing share of the fruits of scientific research and development goes to feed the folly of war. The major part of our taxes are spent on the bills of past wars, on the present economic and ideological war, and as insurance against defeat in future wars. Three major tyrannies have been disarmed at great cost and still another faces us. The science of politics and human relations has made no advance in the thousands of years of which we have record.

We can hardly say that all is well with man even in America. Life is easier, but unrest grows. Leisure increases, but moral stature declines; transport and communication are swift, but suspicion between peoples grows. Man, who should be the lord of creation, is being mastered by matter. Mind has outrun spirit.

Let us examine in a little more detail some of the characteristics of our contemporary life which demonstrate the need for religious faith.

First, let us examine the essentially materialistic philosophy so characteristic of our time, carved by the most efficient tool known to man, the human intellect. With this tool man has penetrated the mysteries of the material universe, freed the minds of men from ignorance and superstition, and created a new physical environment. The successes of science in this area have captured the imagination and the loyalties of many as the only guide to truth. Through the glasses of the scientist man is a physio-chemical system, a machine rather than a soul to be saved or lost. The betterment of men means the improvement of the efficiency of this machine and is to be accomplished by material means. If well housed, well fed, freed of disease, given security, education, and leisure, men should not worry about souls or sins, dreams and aspirations, values. Good sewers and pure water supply are of more concern than a good life.

This philosophy as such is not new in the history of the world. There have always been objectors and agnostics who denied the spiritual nature of man, but never many. Today a materialistic philosophy is held not by a few tough minds but by whole blocs of men. Communism has embraced it completely. And even in our own nation it has become the creed of hosts of men and women by open avowal, quiet assumption or unconscious adoption. Millions of men are beginning to translate their beliefs along this line into action, to live a pagan religion.

The second characteristic of our contemporary life is the intensive specialization of the interests and activities of the individual. The industrial revolution spelled the doom of the skilled craftsman and narrowed the required skill and interest of the worker who assembled in large factories to do a monotonous repetitive task. The worker who tightens a single bolt or solder a single wire connection is not only a figure of fiction but representative of many actual situations. And the white-collar worker is not a stranger to this environment which presents no stimulus much less challenge to his mind. The world as a whole has expanded in knowledge but the world of the individual is often narrow and circumscribed. It is not strange that so many suffer from a kind of intellectual scurvy, a deficiency disorder arising from a restricted intellectual diet. The disease, however, is not so easily cured as the physical disease for pills will not change habits of thought and intellectual outlook.

Even science itself has proceeded down this path and there is no more gullible individual than a scientist outside his own laboratory and discipline. He tends to develop a myopic vision and to the layman his interest seems to be in details remote from what most people consider the real interests and concern of life. In the past he has frequently avoided responsibility for interpreting or passing judgment on his work. He has seen apparently trivial discoveries grow into potent influences in our society and he would rather not make predictions but continue his scientific freedom to pursue the things which interest him.

But the scientist cannot longer dodge his responsibility. As well expressed by Oppenheimer he has known sin. He has seen his greatest conquest of nature applied to an atomic bomb to destroy other men. If the scientist fails to take a hand in the decisions, there are plenty of self-confident and ambitious souls who are not hampered by too much knowledge and who will not hesitate to make decisions for him, not on the basis of scientific experience, or on the basis of moral values, on right and wrong, but on the basis of social and political expediency, or for purely selfish reasons.

What is true of scientists is true of other workers also. They have reason to be disappointed with the ineffectiveness of much of their effort to improve their world. They must seek broader interests than the daily routine of living and making a living. They must participate and assume responsibility for the community in which they live. Specialization in some small area of life must be accompanied by broad interest in all areas of life.

The third characteristic of our generation is a widespread disillusionment and lack of faith, an atrophy of the spiritual life. Man's life should be a trinity of activity, physical, mental, and spiritual. Man must cultivate all three if he is not to be imperfectly developed. Even after thousands of years of education and religious heritage we see far too many of our fellow humans living the life of animals, with sole interest in the physical and sensual and with primitive minds and souls. We find a few religious fanatics who are creatures of instincts and emotion with no guidance from reason. We find many who worship reason and the intellectual life, who appear to normal men as egotistical, selfish, and soulless mechanisms. Jesus said, "Thou shalt love the Lord thy God with all thy heart, and with all thy soul, and with all thy mind. This is the first and great commandment."

The old adage "Knowledge is power" has been found by experience to be only a partial truth. The debasement of knowledge to the service of selfish interests is only too common in our present day. The faith that men's good sense would prevent the misuse of knowledge has been found to be false. One has only to remember how every citizen subordinated and dedicated his special knowledge to the requirements of war, to the devising of more powerful instruments of destruction. Knowledge is power, but not necessarily power for the good of mankind.

The contributions of science to mankind require no defense or apology. These contributions have included not only the devising of powerful tools which can be used to alter the physical environment of man for good or evil, to cure or to kill, but also major contributions to our spiritual life. Science places a high premium on intellectual honesty and on objective truth, truth which can be tested by any man in any age. Science recognizes no arbitrary authority. It does not accept the law of gravitation because of the authority of Newton but because the law of gravitation can be observed and demonstrated as a part of anyone's experience. The ethical ideals of the scientist are high. Notwithstanding all this the scientific discipline itself taken alone is merely the highest development of one aspect of the intellect of man and to cultivate it alone and to exalt it to the status of a religion or philosophy of life is as monstrous as to cut off one's arms, or to destroy the gifts of sight and hearing.

There is another area into which science cannot penetrate with its cold and sharp tools, the area of human emotions, desires, purposes, values, feelings of beauty and ugliness, of right and wrong, of love and hate. "It is the nemesis of the struggle for exactitude by the men of science", remarked a great biologist, Dr. H. S. Jennings, "that leads him to present a mutilated, merely fractional account of the world as a true and complete picture." You can no more analyze these imponderables by scientific methods, said Eddington, than you can extract the square root of a sonnet. Just as in science the elemental reasoning of animals has risen to lofty genius, so may these other aspects ascend from beastly emotionalism to the lofty dreams and aspirations of those a little lower than the angels. Are these workings of the human spirit only illusion or do they herald a report of something deeper, of truth which may be the foundation of a high philosophy of life? Upon the answer which man makes will depend what sort of man he is and can become and what the world is like which he will build.

Perhaps many of you feel that I have given a pessimistic view of our American life, subordinating many of the characteristics of our kindhearted, impulsive, friendly fellow citizens. Perhaps you feel that we are a Christian nation because our institutions, our charities, our generosity, and our slogans of service are consistent with the teachings of Jesus, that these matters of philosophy, of faith, of aspiration are so intangible that they are of no practical importance. If you do, I fear that you too are too typical of our citizenry and that you too need to reconsider the importance of religious faith and practice in your life. You too in the language of the old-time evangelist need to believe on the Lord Jesus Christ and be saved. Why then is religious faith and practice important?

First, because a vital religious faith enables one to have power over any conceivable situation. "Yea, though I walk through the valley of the shadow of death, I will fear no evil; for thou art with me; thy rod and thy staff they comfort me." "Thou shalt not be afraid for the terror by night, nor by the arrow that flieth by day, nor for the pestilence that walketh in darkness, nor for the destruction that wasteth at noonday." "Oh my Father, if this cup may not pass away from me, except I drink it, thy will be done." Whether illness of oneself or loved one, loss of business or personal possessions, or whatever calamity or good fortune, faith can guide your course. Like the gyro compass on the airplane or ship which maintains a fixed reference point undisturbed by the tumultuous storm, religious faith gives a guide in times of mental anxiety and confusion.

We live in a big complicated world and we are affected by shifting and conflicting forces. How to do the right and proper and wise thing in a situation is something that we must know to have power. You want sharpness and keenness to come into your brain; you want courage and strength to make decisions and carry them through. This is the secret. Yield yourself to God. "The Kingdom of God is within you." You do not need to hunt it from the outside, it is within you, just release it. You shall receive power. As the electric motor is powerless without contact with the source of power, so are you without laying hold of the spiritual power source. Sounds simple, doesn't it? You have been defeated in some situation. You have been educated, you have ability, you work hard, but you are defeated by worry, anxiety and frustration. Establish the contact through faith.

In the last analysis the thing that brings power into human lives is something the preachers have been talking about since the beginning of Christian history, namely conversion. Ye must be born again. It means that an individual recognizes his mistakes, his weakness, his insufficiency, perhaps his defeat, realizing that he has no power of his own to change himself and so yields himself wholeheartedly and completely to God. The power of faith is the only power that can change human nature.

Not only will religious faith make us the captains of our souls and master of our lives, but it will lead us to practice that Christian relationship of brotherly love with our fellowman that is so sadly needed in our society today. The bearing of one another's burdens voluntarily is the great lubricant which will make the wheels of our society turn with less friction and heat. We are our brother's keeper and we do have an accountability to use our talents unselfishly to add to the spiritual development of mankind. What a pity that we have found no way to accumulate stores of good will and Christian character as we can accumulate scientific knowledge in books and libraries.

Knowledge piles on knowledge to make an ever-increasing store. But moral accomplishment seems so personal and perishable. We can start with the spiritual development of our ancestors, of Moses, of David, and of Jesus of Nazareth, but so few do. The practitioners and research workers aiming to develop a higher spiritual level of a country or civilization are unfortunately few even in comparison with the educators and scientists.

Unused and neglected talents are lost. But the measure to which a man is gifted, to the same measure is he accountable. We often covet our neighbor's 100 talents as if we could have them without obligation, without responsibility. Some give their physical labor and skill, some their intellectual skill, some few their interest, their heart and soul in the enduring cause of ministering to the needs of mankind. Our American life needs many more devoted men of faith to ease the burden of the world, and to advance the spiritual level of community, city, nation, and world.

A religious faith is essential to our American life to restore our perspective on values and to enable us to lay hold on those things which are eternal, and thus of permanent value. Our materialistic philosophy results from an improper assessment of the values in material things. We thought that money, houses, food, automobiles, motion pictures, radio, television would make us happy. The awakening for many has been rude. We thought that our dollars would retain their value over extensive periods; we thought the religion of our fathers and grandfathers would suffice for us. But like their furniture, their modes of transportation, and their amusements, the value of their religious faith to us has declined to nearly zero. Only a faint nostalgia, a memory of their confident faith remains. We find that we must build this faith anew in our lives; that we must work and struggle and apply our knowledge and skills to the problems of our day. We discover that religious faith requires nurture, that it dies unless used, that we too must seek the fountain of everlasting life. We too must not only echo the age-old song, "O that I knew where I might find Him but must set out on the search." "Seek ye the Lord while He may be found, call ye upon Him while He is near." We must earn our heritage anew. Will a man say because he knows us that there is no better way of living than following Christ?

I close with the story of an experience in a Scottish Church. A visiting university professor of public speaking was attending morning service with his host. He was asked to recite the 23rd Psalm and the old pastor gave his permission. He did so with beauty of diction and exquisite impressiveness and the congregation was visibly moved. Then someone asked the minister also to repeat the Psalm and he did so with such feeling and emotion that when he concluded there was hardly a dry eye in the church.

After the service when walking home, the professor was asked by his friend if he had noticed the difference in the effect on the audience. "Yes," he said, "I did. You see I knew the Psalm but he knows the Shepherd."

                        Hugh L. Dryden, Local Preacher
                        Calvary Methodist Church

Washington, D. C.
March 12, 1950

Index

Index

Advanced Research Projects Agency (ARPA): 12
Air Force, U.S.: 10, 12
Air Force-Navy-NACA Research Airplane Committee: 10
Allen, H. Julian: 11, 13
Ames Aeronautical Laboratory: 8-9, 11
Ames, Joseph: 2, 8
Anemometer: 4
Apollo Program: 15, 18
Army, U.S.: 12, 14
    Ballistic Missile Agency: 14
Army Air Forces, U.S.: 7
    Scientific Advisory Group: 6-7
Arnold, Henry H.: 6-7

Baltimore City College: 1
Baltimore, Maryland: 1
Bat Missile: 5-6
Blagonravov, Anatoly A.: 14
Braun, Wernher von: 6, 13, 14
Briggs, Lyman: 3
Brooks, Overton: 16 ill.
Bush, Vannevar: 5

California Institute of Technology: 14

D-558-1: 10
D-558-2: 10
Doolittle, James: 12
Dornberger, Walter: 6-7
Dryden Flight Research Center: 20. See also NACA High Speed Flight Station and the other early names listed there.
Dryden, Hugh Latimer: 2 ill., 3 ill., 7 ill., 9 ill., 12 ill., 16 ill., 19 ill.
    Academic career: 1-2
    Aerodynamic research: 3-5
    Aerodynamic Theory, contribution to: 5
    "Air Forces on Circular Cylinders" (doctoral dissertation): 2
    "Airplanes: An Introduction to the Physical Principles Embodied in their Use" (masters thesis): 2
    Awards and recognition: 4-5, 7, 20
    Career: 2-3, 4-5, 8, 9, 13
    Character and qualities: 1, 12, 13-14, 17
    Death: 20
    Engineering projects: 4
    Final illness: 17-20
    Life in general: 1, 20
    Negotiations with the Soviet Union: 14
    Religiosity: 1, 4
    "Turbulence and the Boundary Layer": 5, 20
Dryden, Hugh Latimer, Jr. (son): 4
Dryden, Leslie (brother): 1

Dryden: Mary Libbie Travers (wife): 3
Dryden, Mary Ruth (daughter): 4
Dryden, Nancy (daughter): 5
Dryden, Raymond (brother): 1
Dryden, Samuel Isaac (father): 1
Dryden, Zenovia Hill Culver (mother): 1

Echo 1: 15
Eisenhower, Dwight D.: 12
Empire State Building: 4
Explorer 1: 14
Explorer 6: 15

F-1 rocket engine: 14

Gagarin, Yuri: 18
Gemini Project: 18
Gilruth, Robert: 11, 13
Glennan, T. Keith: 13, 15
Goddard Space Flight Center: 14

House Select Committee on Astronautics and Space: 12

Jacobs, Eastman: 9
Jet Propulsion Laboratory (JPL): 14
Johns Hopkins University: 1-2
Johnson, Lyndon B.: 20
Jones, Robert T.: 9
Journal of the Institute of the Aeronautical Sciences: 9

Kármán, Theodore von: 6-7, 7 ill.
Kennedy, John F.: 15, 18
Kerr, Clark: 19
Kuethe, A. M.: 3

Langley Memorial Aeronautical Laboratory: 8, 11, 16
Lewis, George W.: 8, 9
Lewis Flight Propulsion Laboratory: 9
Lockspeiser, Ben: 7 ill.
Lodge, Henry Cabot: 14

Massachusetts Institute of Technology (MIT): 5, 6
Mercury Project: 11, 15, 18
Munk, Max: 9
Muroc Flight Test Unit (later, Dryden Flight Research Center): 9

NACA High Speed Flight Station: 9, 16. See also NASA Flight Research Center, Muroc Flight Test Unit, Dryden Flight Research Center.
National Advisory Committee for Aeronautics (NACA): 2, 5, 8-11, 10 ill., 11 ill., 12
    Aeronautical research: 8-11
    Space Research: 10-11

National Aeronautics and Space Act: 12
National Aeronautics and Space Administration (NASA): 12-20
    Cooperation with the Soviet Union: 14
    Space efforts: 13ff.
    Ten Year Plan: 14
NASA Flight Research Center: 17
National Bureau of Standards (NBS): 2-5, 7-8
National Defense Research Committee (NDRC): 5
Navy, U.S.: 5
New York Times: 15-16

Office of Scientific Research and Development (OSRD): 5

Pickering, William: 13
Pilotless Aircraft Research Station: 9, 11
Pioneer 5: 15
Pocomoke City, Maryland: 1
Prandtl, Ludwig: 4

Quarterly of Applied Mechanics: 9

Rowe, A.P.: 7 ill.

Saturn booster: 14
Seamans, Robert C.: 19 ill.
Silverstein, Abe: 13
Soviet Union: 14 See also Sputnik.
Sputnik: 12
Stack, John: 9
Stever, H. Guyford: 13
Symington, W. Stuart: 10

Tiros 1: 15
Toward New Horizons: 7-8

V-1 cruise missile: 7
V-2 ballistic missile: 7
Van Allen, James A.: 13
Vanguard Project: 12, 14
Variable sweep wing: 16
Victory, John F.: 5

Webb, James E.: 16 ill., 18, 19 ill.
Weick, Fred: 9
Where We Stand: 7
Whitcomb, Richard: 9
Wiesner, Jerome: 15
    Wiesner Report: 15-16
Wind tunnels: 2, 3-4, 8 ill., 8, 10, 16, 17
Worcester County, Maryland: 1
World War I: 2
World War II: 5-7, 10

X-1: 10
X-2: 10
X-3: 10
X-4: 10
X-5: 10, 16
X-15: 10, 11, 16-17

YF-92A: 10
Yeager, Charles E.: 9-10

About the Author

Michael H. Gorn is Associate Editor, Smithsonian History of Aviation Book Series, and Research Collaborator, Smithsonian Institution, National Air and Space Museum. He is the author of several books, articles, and reviews in aerospace history, including *The Universal Man: Theodore von Kármán's Life in Aeronautics* (Smithsonian Institution Press, 1992) and *Harnessing the Genie: Science and Technology Forecasting for the Air Force, 1944-1986* (Government Printing Office, 1988). He is working on a full-length biography of Hugh Dryden under contract with the Smithsonian Institution Press. It is provisionally entitled "Skyward: The Life of Hugh L. Dryden of NASA." Dr. Gorn earned his B.A. (1972) and M.A. (1973) degrees in history at the California State University at Northridge and his Ph.D. degree, also in history, from the University of Southern California (1978).

Monographs in Aerospace History

This is the fifth publication in a new series of special studies prepared under the auspices of the NASA History Program. The *Monographs in Aerospace History* series is designed to provide a wide variety of investigations relative to the history of aeronautics and space. These publications are intended to be tightly focused in terms of subject, relatively short in length, and reproduced in inexpensive format to allow timely and broad dissemination to researchers in aerospace history. Suggestions for additional publications in the *Monographs in Aerospace History* series are welcome and should be sent to Roger D. Launius, Chief Historian, Code ZH, National Aeronautics and Space Administration, Washington, DC, 20546. Previous publications in this series are:

Launius, Roger D. and Gillette, Aaron K. Compilers. *Toward a History of the Space Shuttle: An Annotated Bibliography.* (Number 1, 1992)

Launius, Roger D. and Hunley, J. D. Compilers. *An Annotated Bibliography of the Apollo Program.* (Number 2, 1994)

Launius, Roger D. *Apollo: A Retrospective Analysis.* (Number 3, 1994)

Hansen, James R. *Enchanted Rendezvous: John C. Houbolt and the Genesis of the Lunar-Orbit Rendezvous Concept.* (Number 4, 1995)